REFORMING
INFANT BAPTISM

REFORMING INFANT BAPTISM

Editor: Clifford Owen

Hodder & Stoughton

LONDON SYDNEY AUCKLAND TORONTO

British Library Cataloguing in Publication Data
Reforming infant baptism.
1. Church of England. Infant baptism
I. Owen, Clifford
265.12

ISBN 0-340-52562-2

All quotes are taken from the New International Version
© International Bible Society

Published by Hodder and Stoughton,
a division of Hodder and Stoughton Ltd,
Mill Road, Dunton Green, Sevenoaks, Kent TN13 2YA
Editorial Office: 47 Bedford Square, London WC1B 3DP

Photoset by Rowland Phototypesetting Ltd,
Bury St Edmunds, Suffolk

Printed in Great Britain by Clays Ltd, St Ives plc

Contents

1

Foreword

The Background to Present Reform
by
Clifford Owen

Rector of Clifton upon Teme,
Lower Sapey
and the Shelsleys
(*Diocese of Worcester*)

1

Foreword

The Background to Present Reform

In January 1983 I was cleaning my shoes in the kitchen of the curate's house over an old copy of the *Church Times*! As fortune would have it, it happened to be open at the correspondence columns. My attention was drawn by a letter headed 'Time to grasp the nettle of infant baptism?' The letter was from a clergyman in the North of England, who very briefly explained why he believed the time had now come to make a serious decision about how the Church of England was going to administer infant baptism.

This letter drew an immediate response from me. Some years previously I had come to the conclusion that infant baptism, if it is practised at all, needs to be administered under much clearer conditions and after a longer period of instruction. I was not alone in this conviction, but my dilemma lay in how to take any serious steps to pursue the matter. I had heard of clergy resigning their livings over the issue, but that didn't satisfy me. I believed in the Church of England as part of God's purposes sufficiently to believe that a long process of reform was necessary in the matter. I reached the conclusion that if baptismal reform was needed then a movement was necessary to effect it, and so I wrote back. Unfortunately I received no reply.

A year later when General Synod elections came round I wrote again, this time to all the prospective candidates asking their views on the state of infant baptism. All replied in a politely broad way, but it was obvious that no moves of reform would come from the newly elected in Synod. In the end I sent the *Church of England Newspaper* a letter to which I refer later in this book. The ensuing correspondence ran on for several weeks and eventually the editor drew it to a close and opened a series of articles on the doctrine of infant baptism by a respected evangelical theologian. These articles I presumed were intended to lay the topic to rest effectively with the quiet insinuation of: 'we have been round this course several times before: here is the last word!'

However, after the series of articles closed there was published a counter article from a west country incumbent, Alan Wright of All Saints', Taunton. In this radical article, Alan Wright proposed the far-reaching step that the time had come for the Church of England to declare believers' baptism as the norm within the Church of England and that infant baptism should be relegated to the shadows.

Within minutes of reading this article I found myself on the telephone to Taunton putting to Alan Wright my thought that despite his article the only way forward for baptismal reform was via a movement. As a result of my 'phone call and others it was agreed to hold a meeting for those interested in forming such a movement. So it was that in October 1986 seven of us gathered at Christchurch, Bayston Hill, Shrewsbury to discuss the matter of the future of infant baptism in the Church of England. Two of the seven were from the Church in Wales. At the end of that day the five from the Church of England, including two laymen, signed a statement initiating MORIB: The Movement for the Reform of Infant Baptism. The title summed up what we felt was the perceived need: that infant baptism should be administered under much tighter conditions. It was not so much a case of abolishing the rite for infants, but of drawing out from the parents a sharper understanding and a firmer promise of commitment for the Christian upbringing of the infant. We declared that believers' baptism should become the norm[1] within the Church of England. (This statement was never intended to indicate that infant baptism was to be ruled out, but that the baptism of those able to answer for themselves should be seen as the norm.) This statement, however, led to considerable discussion at the first meeting of the MORIB committee in February 1987. It was voiced that whilst there was considerable ground support for baptismal reform within the Church of England, particularly among the clergy, a number of people would be concerned if they thought that any movement sought to oust the practice of baptising infants. Accordingly the MORIB committee amended its stated aims by the substitution of the words 'that baptism be seen to be the sacrament ordained by Christ for those who wish to be members of his church' (A.S.B. page 212). The use of the language of the Alternative Service Book sought to confirm not only Anglican allegiance, but also something of the spirit of sane reform which produced the A.S.B.

Amongst a number of other activities and projects which the newly born movement looked at, some kind of publication was suggested and this is where the idea of an essay symposium arose. Originally some seven or eight contributions were solicited, but the idea took a back seat as the pace of events quickened and further publications on baptism in book and press came out (see Bibliography). This present collection is a 'privatised' version of the original idea and is not an official promotion of the Movement for the Reform of Infant Baptism. It contains four contributions: Alan Wright's apologia, Bishop Colin Buchanan's history of the atomisation of infant baptism, my own summary of reform since 1940, and a postscript from Roger Godin, lay baptismal reformer in General Synod.

Alan Wright could best be described as a neo-Baptist or a crypto-Baptist within the Church of England. He is far from being the first, and almost certainly not the last, for there are many like him, but generally speaking they keep their heads down. In days gone by such men might have quietly slipped over to the Baptist Churches but Alan, like Christopher

Wansey before him, feels that his love for and commitment to the Church of England compels him to press for reform. Neo-Baptists seldom get ordained as such, but quietly come to that position on baptism through the rigours of years of pastoral practice. Alan, ordained, has in recent years reached a point where in good conscience he feels unhappy about baptising any more infants. This creates a problem for the Diocesan Bishop of course who has to find someone else to carry out the task of the institutional church. (Ought not this particular problem to be looked at in a wider context of Canon Law? Canon B22. 2 was originally intended as a 'conscience clause'.)

Alan has also in recent days moved into the controversial area of 're-baptism' by expressing a wish to be baptised as an adult and has pressed for a theology and liturgy which would legitimise such a 'supplementary' baptism.[2] This phenomenon is not new, but Alan's undoubted courage and integrity have required him to raise this issue publicly.

In part his dilemma stems from the fact of his Billy Graham decision at Harringay in 1954, which left him in confusion over his christening. In his own words:

> In one sense I have been stuck in this dilemma ever since. Even today, more than thirty-five years on from that life changing event, I feel that I have heard and understood the words of Peter to 'repent and be baptised', but have been denied the possibility of entering into their reality by an event that took place without my consent, at a time when I had been baptised without repenting. At the age of fifteen years I had repented, but was denied my birthright by the teaching and discipline of my church. My christening effectively denied me the chance of discovering for myself what it meant to be 'buried with him through baptism' (Romans 6:4). In the recent past I have tried again to make sense of this experience, and to reconcile the teaching and practice of the New Testament with that of the Church of England today (Personal Correspondence).

Alan Wright's essay is the fruit of this dilemma. It was written originally on sabbatical leave at St Deniol's library,

Hawarden (as was my own!) and was intended to be a booklength composition entitled: 'A Parish Priest looks at Baptism: A fresh scriptural look at the sacrament'. His chapter is an edited version of that original work.

Bishop Colin Buchanan needs little introduction. The former Principal of St John's College, Nottingham is the barely-concealed hero of numerous theological students and clergy who have been indebted to him for his enthusiastic and infectious leadership over many years. As author of copious Grove Booklets, former member of the Church of England's Liturgical Commission, and writer on liturgy, Colin's professional touch is not in doubt and will quickly be discovered in his essay. He writes here as a long-standing baptismal reformer and offers a useful and sober historical appraisal of the atomisation of infant baptism. All of us who would seek to reform baptism should take note of what he writes. It was a footnote in one of his latest Grove booklets (Grove Worship Series 98, *Policies for Infant Baptism* p. 5) that first drew my attention to the fact that he was aware of the existence of MORIB and that his suspicions had been aroused as to our motives!

After an initially abrasive entry into the first MORIB Conference at Shrewsbury in May 1988 as a main speaker followed by a crisp luncheon discussion in Birmingham with the MORIB committee, Colin agreed to become MORIB President and has given quiet inspiration to us since.

It is only fair to state that we have discovered that the gulf between the preferred abolitionists and those who are happy to go on baptising babies under tighter conditions has at times seemed large. One of my greatest fears was that in this present publication we might see a Bruno–Tyson syndrome between Alan Wright's essay and Bishop Colin's. Such has not happened. Grove Booklet 24 *Infant Baptism under Cross-examination* by David Pawson and Colin Buchanan has already covered most of that ground and an action re-play here would not add too much. What is required now is a new in-depth look at some entrenched positions and a plea for honesty and integrity.

Roger Godin is a management consultant from Surbiton. From its inception except for a short period he has been a lay member of the General Synod of the Church of England: first for London Diocese and in the recent Synod for Southwark. In 1988 he introduced a private member's motion asking for a working party to produce a report for Synod on the question of 'apparent indiscriminate infant baptism'.[3] It is about this work that he writes here, an epilogue. His interest in baptismal reform was quite independent of MORIB's work but in recent days he has become a member of that group and is now its Vice-Chairman.

I can see three very important contexts in which infant baptism as commonly practised in the Church of England deserves a fresh look.

The first is the now almost historical context of charismatic renewal. Most, but not all of the band of baptismal reformers place themselves within the renewal camp. The inner disturbance seems to come from deep within. The Holy Spirit seems to have been compelling this question upon us. Baptismal reform is the last thing that I would have chosen to get involved with, but somehow it seems high on the Holy Spirit's agenda. The controversial end of the renewal spectrum is the question of attempts to find a rite for immersion in water as an adult, whilst leaving the validity of his or her infant christening intact. On this score both Alan Wright, with his grave doubts about the efficacy of infant baptism at all, and Colin Buchanan with his 'brinkmanship' renewal of vows with immersion are possibly on the same pitch and maybe (just) on the same side.

The second context is the ecumenical. Baptism is an ecumenical sacrament and any attempt to cling to, or reform the sacrament in a one-denominational camp, ignoring the ecumenical context is likely to be distortive. Those of us who have worked for some years in Local Ecumenical Projects know all too well the confusion and hurts that can occur over differing understandings of initiation within one congregation.

It is worth noting some lines from *Christian Initiation and Church Membership*, the report of the British Council of Churches Working Party on the theology and practice of Christian initiation and church membership: '. . . excessive emphasis on the completeness of sacramental initiation presses in the direction not only of a distorted understanding of sacramental efficacy, but also of a spiritually static view of the reality of membership' (page 25). When our discussions are looked at from ecumenical perspectives, some of our cherished sticking-points tend to rock a little at the base.

The third and arguably the most important context for looking at the administration of baptism is the evangelistic one. The Churches are committed to a Decade of Evangelism and already the groundwork is being done to make the last decade of the century the period of significant advance. If we are serious about making disciples, then infant baptism screams from the roof-tops for a complete overhaul. The choice at face value is a simple one: are we to continue to try and evangelise the baptised or baptise the evangelised?

2

A Parish Priest Looks at Infant Baptism
by
Alan Wright

Vicar of All Saints', Taunton

2

A Parish Priest Looks at Infant Baptism

The Origins of Christian Baptism

The problem is that those who ought to know cannot agree. Certainly baptism was part of the rite by which a Gentile convert became a Jew. This proselyte baptism, as it is called, was not the means by which a person became a Jew: a Gentile became a Jew through an act of faith that was sealed by male circumcision. The proselyte bath seems to have been more concerned with the ritual purification of the new Jew so that he could share in the benefits of the People of God. It was not a total immersion as we would understand it, but was self-administered – a bathing in fact – in the presence of two witnesses, who recited parts of the Torah (the Law) as this took place, and with gallons of water specified, to make sure that the water got to every part of the body! It is true that over the years the baptism part of the ceremony became more and more important – possibly because of the preponderance of women converts, but this does not seem to have happened until after the Christian church had become established. In fact it is possible that Christian baptism influenced proselyte baptism, rather than vice versa. All that can be said for certain is that at the time that the Christian church was becoming established there occurs the first clear reference to proselyte baptism as an established practice. However, there seem to be as many, if not more, differences rather than similarities between proselyte baptism and Christian baptism and certainly no incontrovertible connection between the two.

Another development that had taken place in the Jewish

church by the time of Christ was the establishment of a number of religious sects with an emphasis on separation and personal holiness, and with frequent washings, lustrations, or baptisms, as part of their ritual. In the case of some of these sects, the washings occurred daily and possibly two or three times a day. It seems likely that the initial baptism during the ceremony by which a person became a member was of special significance. It is also true that there was a close connection between personal holiness and efficacy of the baptisms, but there is still a remarkable gap between their practices and the proclamation of John the Baptist of a once and for all baptism for the repentance of sins, in preparation for the coming of the Messiah, let alone a clear tie-up with Christian baptism. In the end I personally do not feel qualified to judge whether there is a direct connection between proselyte baptism, baptising sects of the Jordan Valley, and John the Baptist's baptisms, with Christian baptism. I believe it is sufficient that reputable theologians cannot agree on the correct interpretation of the facts to make it very dangerous to put any weight on arguments relying on such a tie-up. So I turn to scripture.

I note that St John the Baptist features prominently at the beginning of all accounts of the life and ministry of Jesus. St Mark and St John effectively begin their gospels with the story of John the Baptist. Not only that, but it seems to be clear that Jesus began his ministry in very much the same mould as John.

Both Jesus and John came from the desert to begin their ministry – for example St Matthew records: 'In those days John the Baptist came, preaching in the Desert of Judea' (Matt. 3:1) and then later tells us: 'Then Jesus was led by the Spirit into the desert' (Matt. 4:1) and later again: 'From that time on Jesus began to preach' (4:17). Secondly both began by baptising; or rather, as far as Jesus was concerned, initially his disciples were baptising other followers (John 4:1,2) possibly just as John was doing. True, St John is the only Gospel writer to record this; he also records that Jesus took his followers away from Judea, possibly in order to prevent any seeming competition between John and his own disciples. Thus although Jesus soon effectively put a stop to the practice of his followers baptising others, it would seem that, as well as being baptised himself, the early days of his ministry were marked by his disciples baptising others, following the same pattern as John's ministry.

Thirdly, the message that Jesus preached was also the same as John's. St Matthew even expresses it in the same words; both Jesus and John the Baptist are quoted as preaching: 'Repent, for the kingdom of heaven is near' (Matthew 3:2; 4:17). This repentance was clearly a matter for the individual.

There are those who would claim that an emphasis on personal repentance is twentieth century intrusion on a New Testament pattern of family relationships. However, we read in Psalm 49: 'No man can redeem the life of another . . . the ransom for a life is costly, no payment is ever enough' (verses 7–8). Ezekiel makes it quite clear that even the most righteous person can do nothing to save others, 'they could not save their own sons or daughters' (Ezekiel 14:18). While it is true that the family has always been of central importance in Judaism, it is also true that John the Baptist's call was for individuals to come to repentance, and to mark their repentance by individual baptism. Similarly from the beginning of His ministry Jesus constantly challenged the individual to repentance. He prophesied indeed that far from coming to faith as a family unit, families would be divided by the Gospel (Luke 12: 49–53). Both John and Jesus preached a Gospel of individual repentance, and individual commitment – John a commitment to the godly community waiting for the Messiah, and Jesus to himself as Messiah.

It is interesting therefore to note both the basic similarities and the essential differences between the baptism of John and that of Jesus. The word 'to baptise' as used in scripture always seems to refer to a total immersion. Certainly accounts of proselyte baptism and the baptisms of the Qumran Community and similar sects, were by total immersion or a bathing that was equivalent.[1]

John's baptism took place in the Jordan, and it seems likely that his baptism would be the same as all others. Indeed, the accounts of the baptism of Jesus refer to his 'coming up out of the water' (Mark 1:10) which seems to be consistent with his emerging from under the water. It is clear too from Paul's referring to our being buried with Christ in baptism (Col. 2:11,12) that Christian baptism was by immersion. The earliest Christian churches all had sizeable pools in their baptisteries, suitable for the candidate to walk down into. It is interesting to note that medieval fonts are invariably big enough for the total immersion of even the biggest of babies. Our present day fonts are a much later innovation.

Not only were both Jewish and Christian baptisms by total immersion, but both demanded repentance from the person being baptised. Interestingly there seems to be no suggestion that baptism plays any part in actually changing a person as far as John's baptism is concerned. When he saw Jewish leaders coming to him to be baptised, he told them to produce 'fruit in keeping with repentance' (Matt. 3:8). He spoke of his baptising 'with water for repentance' (Matt. 3:11), but John's baptism seems to have little or no sacramental aspect to it. It is a sealing, a marking, of a person as a sign that they have repented, and that they are joining with John in preparing to receive the Messiah (Matt. 3:3). The Gospel writers talk of 'a baptism of repentance for the forgiveness of sins' (Luke 3:3). With our teaching of the sacramental quality of the act of baptism, we might be inclined to associate the forgiveness with the act of baptism. At the time of John, no form of baptism was seen in that way; even in the baptising sects, spiritual cleansing came primarily through the individual being right with God.[2] It is likely that John would have been surprised at our separating the two parts, that the inward turning to God in repentance and the outward sign of baptism are simply meant to go hand in hand. Clearly his attitude to the Pharisees and Sadducees shows that he wanted nothing to do with a baptism that was an outward demonstration, but had no inward reality to it; there was to be no baptism without a genuine repentance.

This then is where Jesus began. His preaching picked up John's message, and although his ministry took him to the people of Israel in a variety of places, and also to some of those outside the house of Israel, his message was addressed first of all to those who had accepted John's baptism. Indeed, he set us an example by being baptised himself, so let's spend some time looking at that baptism. There is an apparent contradiction in Jesus being baptised by John, as he was without sin; he had no need of repentance. St Matthew records John's reluctance to baptise Jesus, and his awareness of Jesus' superiority, and his authority over him (Matt. 3:13–15). However, the baptism of John clearly had a wider purpose than being the outward sign marking the inward turning of the individual. Although there is no evidence to suggest that the person who was baptised by John would regard himself as a member of a distinct new community (in sharp contrast with Christian baptism), there would certainly be a sense in which the person who was baptised was identified with that growing band of Jews who were preparing for the coming of the Messiah, and whose repentance and baptism was largely directed to that end. It seems therefore, to have been Christ's desire to be identified with this body, the righteous Jews who were responding to the authentic voice of God through his prophet John the Baptist, that led to his being baptised at the hands of John. 'Jesus replied, "Let it be so now; it is proper for us to do this to fulfil all righteousness." Then John consented' (Matt. 3:15).

Matthew is the only Gospel writer to record John's hesitation, but all four agree that immediately after Christ's baptism, the Holy Spirit descended upon Jesus in the form of a dove. As I compared the four accounts I found myself modifying my previous idea on what actually happened. It does seem that there was a separation between the act of baptism and the descent of the dove. None of the accounts states that the Spirit came down on Jesus while he was actually being baptised, although St Mark does say the Spirit descended on him like a dove 'as Jesus was coming up out of the water' (Mark 1:10a). St John does not give enough detail for us to be precise, but St Matthew tells us: 'As soon as Jesus was baptised, he went up out of the water. At that moment heaven was opened, and he saw the Spirit of God descending like a dove and lighting on him' (Matt. 3:16). The same separation is seen in St Luke whose account reads: 'When all the people were being baptised, Jesus was baptised too. And as he was praying, heaven was opened and the Holy Spirit descended on Him in bodily form like a dove' (Luke 3:21, 22). The Holy Spirit was *not* sent down upon Jesus when he was baptised by John, but immediately afterwards. Which means that if the actual act of water baptism is the means by which a person receives the gift of the Holy Spirit in Christian baptising, then there is a radical difference between John's baptism of Christ and Christian baptism. Indeed, we need to ask ourselves if it is not more likely that the Holy Spirit, is given *after* baptism, following the pattern of the baptism of Jesus.

While Jesus was with his disciples there appears to have been no need for baptism, which at first sight is surprising, as John is recorded by St Matthew and St Luke as saying: 'He will baptise you with the Holy Spirit and with fire' (Matt. 3:11b; Luke 3:16b), and by St Mark and St John as saying: 'he will baptise you with the Holy Spirit' (Mark 1:8; John 1:33). It is possible that one of the reasons that John the Baptist appears to have second thoughts about Jesus (Luke 7:19) is because he, John, had taught that the Messiah would bring judgement and the power of God – baptising with Holy Spirit and with fire – and Jesus was not even baptising let alone baptising with the Holy Spirit.

The key to understanding this comes both at the end of his ministry and after the death of Jesus. John records that in his last evening before his crucifixion, Jesus prepared his disciples, not only for his death, but for their life after his death (John 15:26). He tried to help them see that his death was in fact necessary, which was why he had become angry with

Peter when Peter tried to persuade Jesus not to go to Jerusalem in order to die (Matt. 16:21–23). And one of the grounds of consolation was that if Jesus went back to his Father, then the Holy Spirit could be sent to the disciples (John 14:26; 16:7 following).

It is clear that the disciples did not understand what this meant, as when Jesus repeated this promise after his resurrection (Acts 1:5) they immediately began to talk about an earthly kingdom (Acts 1:6) – the Golden Age which most Jews believed would be ushered in by the Messiah. It seems clear too that Jesus actually had to leave this earth before the gift of the Holy Spirit could be given. St Luke records in the first and second chapters of the Acts of the Apostles that Jesus, having left instructions for his disciples to wait for the gift of the Holy Spirit, returned to his Father, leaving his disciples behind him on the Mount of Olives. It was ten days afterwards, while they were all together, that the Holy Spirit came upon them. *Then* there was fire. In fact tongues of fire resting upon each one of them – a sign perhaps of their own refining as well as the consuming power of the Holy Spirit. There was fire in their hearts that filled them so full that they bubbled over with excitement – to the extent that when Peter started his sermon he had to apologise for the fact that they appeared to be drunk (Acts 2:15).

There was fire in the belly of the preacher, so that he was not afraid to stand up and tell forth the wonderful works of God, all that God had done to bring salvation to his people.

And that lit a corresponding fire in the hearts of three thousand of those listening to Peter (Acts 2:41). That must have been some sermon!

There is no evidence that the hundred and twenty remaining from the original followers of Jesus felt the need to baptise each other. Whether they had all received John's baptism, and felt that that was sufficient when taken in conjunction with the fact that they had clearly received the promised gift from the Father, or whether the experience of the Holy Spirit in overwhelming them, drenching them in God's love, was sufficient in itself we do not know. What is clear is that on that first Christian Pentecost, on what many would reckon to be the first day of the Christian church, those whose hearts had been touched by God, and who had responded to Peter's preaching were told: 'Repent and be baptised, everyone of you, in the name of Jesus Christ for the forgiveness of your sins. And you will receive the gift of the Holy Spirit' (Acts 2:38). There is no description of what happened, as everyone knew what baptism was about. From then on it is quite clear that all who wanted to become followers of Jesus were baptised in water. In fact, the job of the disciples after Jesus had left the earth is summed up by Jesus in St Matthew's Gospel as: 'go and make disciples of all nations, baptising them in the name of the Father and of the Son and of the Holy Spirit, and teaching them to obey everything I have commanded you' (Matt. 28:19,20). Jesus told his disciples to baptise those who wished to become his followers. On the first day of the Christian church those who wanted to join the Apostles in following Jesus were baptised.

In fact, it is quite clear that, apart from the hundred and twenty on the day of Pentecost, whose baptism in the Holy Spirit may have made water baptism unnecessary, the New Testament knows nothing of a believer who is not baptised. Just as we are called to faith, so we are called to be baptised. 'There is one body and one spirit – just as you were called to one hope when you were called – one Lord, one faith, one baptism; one God and Father of all, who is over all and through all and in all' (Eph. 4:4–6).

It would seem that baptism is absolutely central to being a Christian, but who should be baptised, how it should be done, whether there is just one type of baptism, and what happens when we are baptised, are all questions that need to be answered when looking at the practice of baptism today.

Making Sense of Infant Baptism Today?

One of the fascinating things about reading the four accounts of the life of Jesus is that they are all different. For some people this creates problems. For myself there would be problems if they were all the same. They purport to be either eyewitness accounts of the life of Jesus, or accounts drawn up from the evidence of eyewitnesses. Just as the independent accounts of a car accident given by eyewitnesses will differ in detail – sometimes markedly – so we would expect different witnesses to Jesus to remember different things and to give differing emphasis to the things they remember in common.

St Mark's version of Jesus' last words are thus a little different from those of St Matthew, quoted at the end of chapter seven: 'Go into all the world and preach the good news to all creation. Whoever believes and is baptised will be saved . . .' (Mark 16:15,16).

This then gives us the key to those who are to be baptised: 'Whoever *believes*'. In fact we see that this commitment to belief and faith is present in St Matthew's version, he simply puts it slightly differently: 'go and make disciples of all nations' (Matt. 28:19a). St Luke doesn't recount these instructions, but on the other hand St Luke went on to write 'Part 2' in the Acts of the Apostles, in which he spelt out the details of what happened when the Apostles went out to preach the Good News.

The fundamental evidence concerning what is necessary for a person to become a Christian[3] is found in three basic forms.

Firstly: the Gospels record the teaching that Jesus gave concerning a person becoming a disciple or follower of his.

Secondly: the Acts of the Apostles records the major events concerned with the establishment of the Christian church (which consists of all those who had become followers of Jesus).

Thirdly: the Epistles were written primarily to groups of Christians to assist them in their daily life as Christians and in their understanding of the religion that they had accepted.

Complete commitment

The Gospel writers make it very clear that Jesus demands a complete commitment to himself from anyone who wants to be a disciple of his. This begins with his calling of the disciples. For instance, St Matthew tells us (my italics) 'As Jesus was walking beside the sea of Galilee, he saw two brothers, Simon called Peter and his brother Andrew. They were casting a net into the lake, for they were fishermen. "Come, follow me," Jesus said, "and I will make you fishers of men." *At once they left their nets and followed him*' (4:18–20).

It is a recurrent theme in his teaching. Thus he tells the man who says that he will catch up with him after he has settled the affairs of his father's death: 'let the dead bury their own dead' (Matt. 8:22b). He tells the rich young man: 'sell your possessions and give to the poor, and you will have treasure in heaven. Then come, follow me' (Matt. 19:21b). Jesus calls for his disciples to put their complete faith and trust in him.

In St John's Gospel Jesus speaks of this in terms more directly applicable to our present situation.

Jesus tells us: 'Whoever believes in the Son has eternal life' (John 3:36). Note: they *have* eternal life – it begins at conversion, not after death. 'If anyone loves me, he will obey my teaching. My Father will love him and we will come to him and make our home with him' (John 14:23). And again: 'No-one can enter the kingdom of God unless he is born of water and the Spirit' (John 3:5).

Later Jesus says: 'I tell you the truth, he who believes *has* everlasting life' (John 6:47, my italics).

There seems to be a very clear pattern. A person must believe in Jesus and then he will receive eternal life.

However, as I have said earlier, it is also clear that Jesus is talking about something much more radical than mere intellectual consent. There must be a rebirth, an experience that involves a deep spiritual response, and our whole relationship with God will be changed, so that Jesus can talk of himself and the Father making their home in us. This surely is the same sort of total commitment that was required when Jesus called his disciples.

This total commitment is evident in the early days of the Christian church. We read that on the Day of Pentecost: 'Those who accepted his [Peter's] message were baptised', and that: 'They devoted themselves to the apostles' teaching and to the fellowship, to the breaking of bread and to prayer' and: 'All the believers were together and had everything in common' (Acts 2:41,42,44).

This total commitment, this turning away from the past life – necessary for Jew as well as Gentile – is seen very clearly in the Epistles. Paul tells the Christians at Rome that: 'by dying to what once bound us, we have been released from the law so that we serve in the new way of the Spirit' (Rom. 7:6). St Paul clearly sees the process of becoming a Christian as being a dying to the old life, a burial in Christ, and then being raised to new life in him (Col. 2:11,12). In Colossians 2:20 he writes: 'Since you died with Christ to the basic principles of this world . . .' There can be no more complete commitment to Christ than to die with him to all that has gone before.

So, if a person is to become a Christian they must commit themselves to Christ totally and completely. This is the witness of scripture in the whole of the New Testament. This surely is what St Peter meant when, in response to questions asked at the end of his sermon, he told his hearers: 'Repent . . .' There was to be a turning away, a dying to the old life. There was to be a reaching out in faith to Jesus Christ: 'You are all sons of God *through faith* in Christ Jesus' (Gal. 3:26, my italics). This was to be sealed in the waters of baptism, and the new Christian, having died, been buried in the waters of baptism and then raised to new life in Christ Jesus, was filled with the power of the Holy Spirit. 'Repent and be baptised every one of you, in the name of Jesus Christ for the forgiveness of your sins. And you will receive the gift of the Holy Spirit' (Acts 2:38).

Let us pause at this point, and reflect on the vast majority of christenings that take place in the United Kingdom today.

The scene is so familiar. The group around the font. The proud parents. The smiling faces of family and friends. The anxious look on the face of the godmother, trying to do everything properly. The pink bundle in her arms, engulfed in a beautiful white christening gown. It's a lovely scene, especially if it is a bright day, and the baptistery is bathed in colour and the sun streams through the stained-glass windows.

However, if we take off the rose-tinted spectacles and take a good hard look at what is being said, then the scene changes. Quite early in the proceedings, parents and godparents make statements of faith:

> I turn to Christ
> I repent of my sins
> I renounce evil[4]

For the overwhelming majority of parents and godparents these are mere words. Christ seems little more than a figure of fantasy – the centre of the cosy celebrations that are important in December, and little else. Far from turning to him for the strength, grace, guidance, etc. that he is longing to give, the chances are that his name only crosses their lips at times of anger and stress, when their cursing needs some strength.

Many, if not most, of those who play out such cosy charades around the font have little idea of sin. True they have perfectly good consciences, but these function, in the normal way, on the data supplied. And today in this country that data has a remarkably small Christian content. Sin is usually seen as what society frowns on, rather than what offends the Almighty. Thus on telling an unmarried mother that she could not possibly repent of one particular sin while she continued to live with the father of the baby, I was told: 'But everybody does it'! It is a similar story when challenging people over occult practices which they regard as harmless. 'It's good for a laugh.'

And if neither parents nor godparents have any discernible faith, then certainly it is clear that the tiny bundle who is about to be splashed can have no faith at all!

Where then is the faith that is the prerequisite of membership of the Christian church? There were occasions when Jesus healed because of the faith of others. When the paralytic was lowered through the hole that his friends had made in the roof, St Mark tells us: 'When Jesus saw their faith, he said . . .' (Mark 2:5). It is possible to make out a case to support the idea that baptism, like circumcision before it, can be entered into by a child through the faith of his or her father. Something like this must have been at the root of the second century practice of the baptism of a child on the strength of its parents' faith.[5] However, there is no suggestion anywhere that such a baptism can take place on the strength of the faith of anyone else. The necessity of faith for baptism means that it is impossible to justify theologically the current Church of England practice of the indiscriminate baptism of infants. Our present practice is a gross abuse of the sacrament.

In addition, of course, the child is not actually 'baptised' in the Greek sense of the word 'baptizo' – meaning to totally immerse, be completely engulfed in. There seems to be not a shred of evidence that 'baptizo' was ever used to describe a process of sprinkling. (In proselyte baptism water was poured on, but gallons of it were used to make sure that the candidate was thoroughly soaked.) Thus in indiscriminate infant baptism we have a supposed new birth taking place without faith, and a burial in the waters of baptism by means of a shell-ful of water that is sprinkled on. Where is the New Testament sacrament of baptism in all this? I venture to suggest that it might not be there at all.

But what happens if we say 'no' to the christening of children whose parents are outside the church family? Are we not punishing the baby because of the shortcomings of the parents? I am not at all sure that by denying them the waters of baptism we are in reality denying them anything at all.

Firstly, what evidence do we have to support the idea that baptism in itself, divorced from faith, actually achieves anything? I would challenge anyone to spend some time with an average class of five-year-olds, and then separate the baptised from the non-baptised on the external evidence. I have been able to see the difference in character between children brought up in a Christian home and those brought up in a non-Christian one. I have never been able to discern the difference between those who have been christened and those who have not been, amongst children who had been brought up in non-Christian homes. However, it is quite clear from scripture that the process of repentance, conversion, baptism in water and the receiving of the Holy Spirit does bring about a fundamental change in the character of the person concerned (whether they have had a Christian upbringing or not). It was quite clear in Samaria when this process had gone wrong (Acts 8:14–17). Similarly it was quite clear when this change had taken place without the waters of baptism (Acts 10:44–48).

Which brings me to my second point: that water baptism does not automatically bestow the gift of the Holy Spirit. A person can on the one hand receive baptism without there being any sign of a rebirth (Acts 8:9–17), and on the other hand show all the signs of having received the Holy Spirit without having been through water baptism (Acts 10:44–48). (The sign of having received the Spirit indicates incorporation into Christ (1 John 3:24).) This reasoning must apply both to believer's baptism and to infant baptism, if, as the Church of England teaches, the two have the same effect on the individual. Unless the person being baptised is right with God, they may say the right words, but to quote a Free Church pastor: 'It will be no more than a sheep dip!'

There is nothing automatic about a sacrament. We do not receive the gift of eternal life simply by going through the waters of baptism, for salvation comes by grace through faith; 'not by works, so that no-one can boast' (Eph. 2:9). Clearly a baptism without faith is a form of 'works', something that we do; just as clearly we can observe that it seems to have precisely no effect on the life of the person receiving such a baptism.

Thirdly, the decision to deny baptism to the child of

non-believing parents appears to make no difference to the child's development. Indeed it may be a more constructive act by preventing the child later on from falling into the error of believing in the eternal 'insurance policy', namely that christening will eventually get him or her to heaven with no faith needed on their part.

There are two other common reactions from those who were 'done' as babies. On the one hand there are those who assess the claims of Christ and then reject them, deciding not to become Christians. They can be annoyed when they discover that apparently they have been made Christians when they were too young to be consulted. They feel they have been denied their right to say 'no' to the Gospel. On the other hand there are those who come to a living faith, joyfully fulfilling the promises made on their behalf at their christening. However they too can be equally disappointed to be told that they have already been baptised once, and cannot be baptised again. They have repented, they have put their faith and trust in the Lord Jesus. They earnestly desire to follow the New Testament injunction of: 'Repent and be baptised' (Acts 2:38). But christening has apparently denied them the birthright of a newly-born Christian.

However, there is the very real problem that simply to refuse baptism, or to impose conditions that effectively amount to refusal, means that what is often the first contact between young parents and the local parish church is almost totally negative. 'The Vicar wouldn't christen my baby' is what is passed on, despite the fact that what was said was, in effect, 'Yes, I will baptise the baby, but there are certain conditions'. And a refusal to christen the baby is taken quite simply as a rejection of the family concerned.

At All Saints', Taunton we have struggled with this one; painfully aware of the feelings of rejection amongst parishioners, yet believing that to assist parents and godparents to commit perjury in church is not the answer.

Our latest attempt to provide a way forward follows the example of a church in Liverpool Diocese (All Saints',

Stoneycroft). When enquiries are first made, I go to the home concerned to have a brief chat with the parents, and explain that the first thing that we do is to have a Thanksgiving Service for the baby.[6] The service is at a time when the church family will also be present (10.00 a.m.), and the parents are encouraged to bring friends and family to give thanks with them. Thus the first contact between family and church is a positive, welcoming one.

A second interview follows at which some of the obligations of the baptism promises are explained. Most parents accept that they cannot possibly keep the promises themselves unless they are part of a worshipping community, and that their knowledge of the Christian faith is so severely limited that they are in no position to teach their child what it means to be a Christian. It is all set out in the introduction to the Alternative Service Book's 'The Baptism of Children' (p. 243).

> Children who are too young to profess the Christian faith are baptised on the understanding that they are brought up within the family of the Church.
>
> As they grow up, they need the help and encouragement of that family, so that they learn to be faithful in public worship, and private prayer, to live by trust in God, and come to confirmation.
>
> Parents and Godparents, the child whom you have brought for baptism depends chiefly on you for the help and encouragement they need. Are you willing to give it to them by your prayers, by your example, and by your teaching?

And to all this the parents and godparents have to reply: 'I am willing.'

Most parents can see that to give help 'by your prayers, by your example, and by your teaching' involves them having the knowledge to pass on and being prepared to pray regularly, read their Bible regularly, and to attend worship regularly. For many this involves a change of life style that they are not prepared to make, so they do not go forward to baptism, usually being content with what has been done for them in the Thanksgiving Service.

Some however are prepared to go on with what is involved in this first promise in the baptism service. There is no way that I can check whether they are beginning to pray or read their Bibles regularly, but what I can see is whether they have been regular in worship, and whether they have attended one of the baptism preparation courses that we stage at quarterly intervals throughout the year. Only after regular attendance at worship for some months by at least one of the parents, and attendance for the five sessions of the preparation course by both parents, will I go on to baptise the baby, or to give permission for the baptism to take place elsewhere (unless of course the parents are members of the church concerned).

But what about faith? The necessity of faith for baptism is explained as part of the course, and I do all I can to bring parents to the point of faith prior to the christening, but in the end I have to take at face value the willingness of parents to make promises on behalf of their infant.

I am sure that there are many different ways of helping people to act in a responsible way concerning the christening of their babies, and the A.S.B. makes it very clear what some of these responsibilities are.

It is time that parish priests and congregations began to take the responsibilities seriously themselves. How do we expect to be taken seriously as a church when we admit people to membership simply on the grounds that they have asked to become members and live within a certain geographical area?

I believe that it is also time that we thoroughly re-appraised the whole concept of baptising babies at all. It is this issue that I shall now address.

Is Child Baptism Possible?

A few years ago the Good News Crusade came to Taunton. Their fundamental approach was simple: to reach as many people as possible with the Gospel and the love of Jesus. To this end, in addition to the main meetings, they held many 'specialist' meetings. Small groups went into class rooms, attended coffee mornings, spoke at pensioners' clubs, etc. And each week they held a Gospel meeting aimed at children.

I was involved in the planning of the Crusade, and preaching the Gospel to young children was the only part of the Crusade that bothered me. Was it right to put small children under emotional pressure to get them to make the sort of decision that I suspected only an adult could make?

Nevertheless I went to the meetings with three of my children, aged four, ten and twelve years old. The two eldest had already asked Jesus into their lives and were born again Christians, but I was intrigued to see how four-year-old Sarah would react.

The first thing that struck me was that there was no undue pressure put on the children. An enjoyable service, bright choruses, a little drama and a simple, direct presentation of the Gospel. There was of course an altar call and many of the children streamed forward, Sarah included. When she came back we asked her what happened. She was a little disappointed: 'I wanted to give my heart to Jesus, but the lady said to wait till next time.' In fact it was only after going forward on three occasions that Sarah was allowed to make her commitment to Christ. Clearly no undue pressure was involved.

But how can a child make such a decision? I don't know, but I do know that Jesus said that we are to let the little children come to him (Matt. 19:14). He also said that 'anyone who will not receive the kingdom of God like a little child will never enter it' (Mark 10:15). Little children can do just that without having to make the sort of effort that adults often have to make to have a childlike faith. Children often go straight to the heart of the matter, uncluttered as they are by the prejudices and preconceptions that we adults carry around with us.

As far as Sarah was concerned we saw the change in her life. She was never a particularly difficult child, but she became more loving and tractable. A couple of months later her Sunday School teacher remarked on the great change that had taken place in Sarah's life. She was quite clear herself about what had happened and a year or so later volunteered her testimony in church. Very simply, and with little or no prompting from me, she told how, at the age of four and a half (the 'half' was very important!), she had asked Jesus into her life, and what a difference it had made. 'Let the little children come to me . . .' is what Jesus said then, and he says it still today. This is what Sarah did, as many others have done in the past two thousand years.

What then about christenings? Is this not a case of responding to the call of Jesus? I do not believe it is.

First, there is no suggestion in scripture that when Jesus issued this wonderful invitation he was thinking of anything remotely resembling baptism. St John tells us that Jesus did not baptise (John 4:2). When Jesus told his disciples to let the little children come to him it was so that he could bless them and pray for them (Matt. 19:13–15). The incident seems to consist of a direct interaction between Jesus and children who responded to his love. In St Mark's account of this incident Jesus goes on to talk of our response in faith to him. Clearly he was not thinking about an adult responding on behalf of an infant (Mark 10:13–16).

Second, there is not a single reported instance in the whole of the New Testament of a baby being baptised. It seems clear from archaeological evidence that the practice of infant baptism was commonplace, if not the norm, by the second or third century.[7] A case can also be made to suggest that reference to 'households' being baptised would include children, and that Peter's reference to children in Acts 2:39 extends the concept of baptism to babies, (this seems to be stretching things rather a long way!) The fact remains, however, that these are mere suppositions. Indeed, they seem suspiciously like attempts to extend second- and third-century evidence for infant baptism back into the New Testament, where no such evidence exists. I repeat, there is not a single clear, unambiguous, reference to the baptism of a baby in the whole of the New Testament.

Thirdly, baptism demands a response from the person becoming a Christian. How then can baptism be undertaken by a person too young to speak for themselves?

Thus, when Christian baptism was first administered as recorded in Acts 2, repentance was called for. Clearly it is not possible for a babe-in-arms to repent.

At the same time the promise was given that the newly baptised person would receive the gift of the Holy Spirit (Acts 2:38b). This, of course, is what an infant receives at baptism – or so we are told. At this point an independent enquirer, reading the New Testament, but also learning Anglican doctrine, is most likely to conclude that we have a classic case of people using the same language, but investing it with entirely different meanings.

What sort of being is this Holy Spirit? In the Acts of the Apostles, when the Holy Spirit came down on the hundred and twenty in the Upper Room there was first of all a violent wind. This was followed by the well-known candle effect: 'tongues of fire that separated and came to rest on each of them' (Acts 2:3). They then started speaking in tongues (a God-given language that usually cannot be translated, and whose meaning comes as a special dispensation from God, and which seems to be different for every single person who receives this gift). They came out from behind the locked doors (cf. John 20:19,26) and caused so much commotion that before Peter could give the text for his sermon he had to explain that he and his friends were not drunk! (Acts 2:15). Now it does seem to me that this is vastly different from the cosy scene round the font that we imagined above. Has the Holy Spirit changed? Have we changed? Or are we really talking about very different things?

You see, it's all very well to talk about a baby receiving the Holy Spirit at a christening, *but where is the evidence to support this incredible claim*? I personally have never been able to observe any difference in a baby due to its christening, nor any difference between baptised and non-baptised babies that could clearly be attributed to the baptism itself.

The New Testament picture is very different. When a person became a Christian he received the Holy Spirit. When he received the Holy Spirit there was an immediate, observable, change.

The change in the behaviour at Pentecost has already been mentioned. It was only after receiving the Holy Spirit that the disciples were able to exercise the other gifts (e.g. Acts 3:1–10). When something went wrong and baptism was administered but the Holy Spirit was not received, Peter and John seem to have had no difficulty in detecting the difference (Acts 8:14–17). Similarly Simon the magician, whose conversion seems to have come about, at least in part, through the miracles performed by Philip (Acts 8:9–13), on seeing the incredible difference in Christians when they received the Holy Spirit, wanted to buy the power to be able to bestow the Holy Spirit, and was expelled by Peter for his pains (Acts 8:18–24). A scene flashes before the mind's eye. There is a small parish church. The church is packed. In an atmosphere of quiet reverence the Bishop lays his hands on the confirmation candidates one by one. One by one they rise from their knees, bow to the Bishop and return to their pews. As the last person returns to their place an excited onlooker rushes down the aisle crying out: 'Bishop, Bishop, that was fantastic, mind-blowing!!! Here's £10,000 for you if you will give me the power to bestow the gift of the Holy Spirit on others!' It would be incredible – indeed, beyond the imagination. Just as it is entirely unreasonable to take Acts 8 as describing the first confirmation. Simon the magician could *see* the difference in candidates after the laying on of hands, and the difference was so incredible that he wanted the power to do this fantastic thing himself. How often is it possible to see *any* difference in confirmation candidates after confirmation?

In Acts 10 the Holy Spirit was given without the benefit of baptism, so Peter decided to regularise things, and have all those present baptised. He proceeded to the baptism with confidence because those present could see and hear the difference in Cornelius and his household (verses 44–48). This was no hidden gift. In fact, I am not aware of any account in scripture of the Holy Spirit being given to a person in a quiet, hidden way, not observable by others. There would seem then, to be serious objections to the Anglican teaching about the essential reality of baptism and confirmation. What evidence is there to show that the Holy Spirit is in fact given on these occasions? Where in the New Testament does the Holy Spirit have this mole-like behaviour – going underground at a christening, burrowing away unseen for years, and then happily popping up to the surface in adult years. It would be wrong to rely entirely on subjective external evidence; however, how can we persist in maintaining that the Holy Spirit is given when there is little or no external evidence.

Fourthly, there are elements in the New Testament teaching about baptism that make no sense when applied to infant baptism. Paul sees baptism as a burial: 'don't you know that all of us who were baptised in Christ Jesus were baptised into his death? (Rom. 6:3) and 'having been buried with him in baptism and raised with him' (Col. 2:12). How does an infant share in the death of Christ? As an adult I am able to recognise my sins, and in rejecting them die to sin. My death comes at conversion when I repent of my sins and ask Jesus into my life to be my Lord and Saviour. (If I am to be buried in baptism then death must come first, for it is not customary to bury people *before* they die!) Having died to self I can be buried with Jesus in baptism, and rise again to new life, going into the grave as I go under the water, and rising up through the water to new life. What sense can a person sprinkled as an infant make of this? Being unable to speak for myself, I was unable to repent of my sins, and was therefore unable to die to sin. Even if I had been fully immersed, and of course I was not, what value would the experience have been to one of such tender years? Both the inward reality and the outward symbolism of being 'buried with him in baptism' would seem to be denied to the person christened as a baby.

Fifthly it is a truism to say that God has no grandchildren. It is as we accept Jesus for ourselves that we become children of God. So St John tells us: 'Yet to all who received him, to those who believed in his name, he gave the right to become the children of God' (John 1:12) Paul, talking to 'believers' in 2 Cor. 6:18 says: 'I will be a father to you, and you will be my sons and daughters, says the Lord, the Almighty.' We are sons and daughters of God through belief, through faith, and this is not something that our children can inherit from us, just as in the Old Testament righteousness could not be passed on to children (Ezek. 14:20). A person has to come to a point of faith themselves if they wish to become a child of God.

Now, if God cannot have grandchildren, if we become a child of God by putting our faith in him, how is it possible for God to have children by proxy? What right do I have to take such a step on behalf of another person, even if they are very close to me? Certainly when the head of the family came to faith, children were incorporated into the Old Covenant through circumcision on the basis of faith of their parent(s) (Gen. 17:23). However, as a Christian I come under the New Covenant. The Old Covenant was written on stone, and the New Covenant is written on the heart (Heb. 8:10), and we might expect it to work differently. Even in the Old Covenant, circumcision is not the means by which a person becomes a Jew. Abraham became a Jew by putting his faith in God. He received the promise through faith. He entered into a covenant with God while still uncircumcised (Gen. 15:18). That covenant, which Abraham entered into through faith, his descendants would share by virtue of their descent from him: 'To your descendants I give this land . . .' (Gen. 15:18). Thus circumcision for Abraham, and for a convert to Judaism and also for a person who is a Jew by natural descent, is God's sign to mark a person *who is already a Jew*. A Jewish baby is a Jew by birth: circumcision is the sign of what is already true. Similarly baptism serves the same function in the New

Covenant: it is God's sign to mark a person *who has already become a Christian*. And the only way to enter into the New Covenant is for the person wishing to become a Christian to put their faith and trust in Jesus Christ (John 3:16).

The apparent exception would seem to be the household of Abraham, who, after Abraham had entered into a covenant with God, were also circumcised (Gen. 17:23). This is also the case for the families of converts. It would seem then that there might be good precedent for the present practice of infant baptism, where the parent(s) of a baby make promise on his or her behalf.

In fact this is not the case. In the first place in the Old Covenant there were only a few who were circumcised under these circumstances – an exception to the general rule. And it could be said that theirs was in reality also a case of physical descent.

In the second place the family relationships are different. In the Old Covenant, although God dealt directly with Abraham, the promises and covenant are always between God and the whole family. This pattern has always been present in Judaism, and is one of the great strengths of the Jewish faith, that has enabled it to survive centuries of exile and homelessness. In fact, initially Yahweh was seen as a family God, similar to other family gods, but a jealous God who would not tolerate the family worshipping any other gods. When Yahweh called a people to be his through the prophet Moses, he still entered into a covenant with the families of that nation. So on the night of the Passover, when God brought his people, the Jews, out of Egypt, he instructed them: 'each man is to take a lamb for his family, one for each household' (Exod. 12:3b).

Now the New Covenant was announced on the night before Jesus died. After supper he 'took the cup, saying, "This cup is the new covenant in my blood"' (1 Cor. 11:25). And this new covenant was also for a family, *but not the natural family*. Jesus made it quite clear that he was establishing a *new* family, a family of believers. He called men to be with him as a family.

He taught that his teaching would divide the natural family (Matt. 10:35,36). He taught that those who put their faith in him and accepted his teaching were more his family than his mother Mary and her other sons (Matt. 12:48–50). And when he announced his new covenant, it was announced to his new family, the Christian family of believers (Luke 22:20).

In addition, there is no true parallel between the decision of the head of a present-day nuclear family with regard to a christening and the head of the family at the time of Christ. The pattern of behaviour would probably have been similar to that of many present-day primitive societies, namely that the family would have debated the matter, and the decision then pronounced by the head as a result of this deliberation. This pattern is seen in Acts 15, verse 19 when the leaders of the Christian family debated, and at the appropriate point their leader/head (James) pronounced a decision on behalf of all. He says 'It is my judgement,' but the ensuing letters says 'so we all agreed' (Acts 15:25). This is a very different process from that which usually takes place when a baby is christened.

It is therefore clear that a straight parallel cannot be drawn between circumcision and baptism as far as babies are concerned. Baptism is God's seal on the person who has become a Christian. The individual enters the Christian family through faith (Eph. 1:13), and thus baptism is meaningless as as far as a baby is concerned. In fact, the Old and New Covenants are different, and the New Testament, when it comments on them is often concerned, not to stress their similarities, but to stress their differences, and of course the New Covenant is the *fulfilment* of the Old.

If the Old Testament parallel does not support infant baptism, is there any evidence in the New Testament to support the idea that a decision of faith can be taken by one person on behalf of another? In order to answer this question we need to look briefly at the New Testament record concerning baptism.

The basic pattern seems to be that given in Acts 2, verse 38. In response to questions at the end of his sermon, Peter said:

'Repent and be baptised, every one of you, in the name of Jesus Christ for the forgiveness of your sins. And you will receive the gift of the Holy Spirit.' We read in Acts 2 verse 11: 'Those who accepted his message were baptised . . .'

This basic pattern of personal response, personal faith, followed by immediate baptism can also be seen in:

Acts 8:12–13	Conversions in Samaria
Acts 9:1–19	Saul's conversion. (Unusually there was a three-day gap between the conversion and baptism of St Paul: this is the longest recorded gap in the New Testament between conversion and baptism)
Acts 16:29–34	The Philippian jailer and his family
Acts 18:7–8	Crispus and his household
Acts 19:1–7	The twelve at Ephesus

In these five instances we can see very clearly the pattern of personal faith, followed by baptism, and in a number of cases clear evidence also of the baptised people receiving the Holy Spirit.

There are however some instances recorded that don't fit into this pattern.

In Acts 8, verses 9–17, although the pattern of faith followed by baptism is clear, it is also clear that baptism does not automatically bring the bestowal of the Holy Spirit. In this incident at least there had to be a separate laying on of hands. When Peter preached to Cornelius there is no reference to repentance, and the listeners received the Holy Spirit before baptism (Acts 10:23b–48).

The only other occasion where the pattern is not clear is in Acts 16:13–15 where Lydia's faith is clearly spelt out, but no comment is made concerning the faith of her household. This means that we have two possibilities, either they came to a point of faith and this is not mentioned, or they did not, but were baptised on the strength of Lydia's faith. However, in view of the evidence of the rest of the Acts of the Apostles, and in view also of the clear teaching of the New Testament that salvation comes through faith, it seems to me to be perverse to choose the latter option. I personally would assume that in this very brief passage, St Luke has simply omitted to write of the faith of the household.

If there is positive evidence of children being baptised on the strength of the faith of their parents, we ought to find it in passages concerned with the baptism of households. In some instances, the faith of the rest of the household, apart from the head, is documented. Thus in Acts 10 verse 24 we read that the 'relatives and close friends' of Cornelius listened with him to Peter's sermon; we read in verse 44 that: 'the Holy Spirit came on all who heard the message' and then in verse 48: 'So he ordered that they be baptised in the name of Jesus Christ.' The whole household heard the message. They all came to faith. They were all baptised.

Similarly when the Philippian jailer responded to the gospel we read in Acts 16 verse 32: 'Then they spoke the word of the Lord to him and to all the others in his house' and in verse 34 that: 'he was filled with joy because he had come to believe in God – he and his whole family'. I am aware that there is dispute concerning the precise translation of this last verse, but I can see little point in mentioning the fact that the whole household heard the gospel if the baptism was simply on the strength of the faith of the jailer himself. The alternative, that he and his whole family came to faith and were then baptised, is surely much more likely.

In Acts 18 verse 8 we read: 'Crispus, the synagogue ruler, and his entire household believed in the Lord; and many of the Corinthians who heard him believed and were baptised.' Clearly the whole household came to personal faith and then were baptised.

There remains a further brief reference to a household being baptised. In 1 Corinthians 1, verse 16 the passing reference to the baptism of Stephanus is so scanty that it doesn't mention anyone's faith.

So, of the five households mentioned, three come to baptism with the whole household having heard the gospel and coming to faith. The two other somewhat scanty references, do not make any positive statement about the faith of the members of the household. In every case where there is clear detail, it is certain that the household have heard the gospel and responded. In the teaching in the rest of the New Testament the necessity of faith before baptism is also clear. To be asked to believe that the two households where no statement is made about the faith of the members follow a completely different pattern seems to be very strange indeed. Why should they be the odd ones out? I can see no good reason from scripture to suppose that members of households were baptised on the basis of the faith of the head of the household. Indeed the evidence is strongly against such a conclusion. Whether or not there might possibly have been infants in such households who might or might not have been baptised is a speculation that is thus totally irrelevant, as there is no reason to believe that any members were baptised without first making an act of faith.

Unless I have missed some biblical evidence of great weight, it seems to me to be very clear that there is no evidence to support the idea that someone can take the step of faith, necessary in the process of becoming a Christian, on behalf of another person.

My wife and I are quite clear. If we were starting our family now, we would dedicate our infants to God, and as soon as they came to faith (in the case of our children at ages ranging from 4½ years to 8–9 years), then they would be baptised by total immersion.

The tradition of the church is strongly in favour of infant baptism. However as far as I have been able to discover, there is little or no biblical evidence to support this tradition.

Epilogue

1. In view of the fact that the Old Testament records a whole variety of lustration/baptisms/ceremonial washings, is it not

possible that the true parallel lies not between baptism and circumcision, but between one baptism and another baptism?

We see this, for instance, at Sinai as recorded in Exodus 19. The Jews first gave a promise to serve God (verse 8). They were then consecrated through a ceremonial washing (in which one must surely presume that the body was thoroughly washed as well as the clothes). The Lord then came down 'in fire' and only then was the covenant given.

Is this not the pattern of Acts 2 – repentance, water baptism, and receiving the Holy Spirit?

We are told that the significance of circumcision lies in what it represents in the heart of the believer. In Acts we see a dispute over circumcision which is finally resolved in Acts 15, and in which the outward sign of circumcision was deemed to be unnecessary for a Gentile. The inward reality was still, however, vitally necessary, as we see in Romans 3 where Paul deals with the question of circumcision, and is clearly set out in Romans 3, verse 22 where he says: 'This righteousness from God comes through faith in Jesus Christ to all who believe.'

In addition, we do have patterns to follow. Jesus himself was presented at the Temple and dedicated to God. True he was circumcised later, but this we are told is not necessary for Gentile Christians. Many years later he was baptised. Is not this a perfectly good example to follow?

And again, in 2 Timothy, Paul talks of Timothy's upbringing. Clearly this was a Christian one – both his mother and his grandmother were Christians (2 Tim. 1:5). However, when Paul reminds him of the things of value in his upbringing, there is no suggestion of a christening. Instead he points him to the scriptures 'which are able to make you wise for salvation *through faith* in Christ Jesus' (2 Tim. 3:15).

Incidentally, it is a fact that the power of the Holy Spirit, in the form of the gifts of the Spirit quickly died out in the life of the early church, so that a person who was able to exercise such gifts became the exception, rather than the rule, and was designated a 'Saint'. If the evidence of Jeremias and others is accepted it is clear that the practice of infant baptism grew very quickly in those early years. These two phenomena are surely mutually dependent. How can God give the fullness of the Holy Spirit to a tiny infant? They are simply not able to exercise the gifts. It is surely because more and more Christians chose to christen their babies that the gifts of the Holy Spirit died out in the first and second centuries. It is my belief that the custom of baptising infants is largely responsible for a church that lacks the power of the Holy Spirit.

2. If I were to concede that there is a case from scripture to support the idea of baptising the children of believers, for instance, as expressed in 'Covenant Theology', I would want to ask those who held it one simple question, namely: 'Are you prepared to be consistent in holding to and applying this theology?' If such a person were to say 'Yes' to this, I would then ask them when they last baptised a person who had been christened as a baby, but whose parents had no discernible faith. In general in the Church of England those who hold to a covenant theology are highly selective in their use of such a doctrine. They are prepared to teach that a baby can only become a Christian through the faith of the parents, but they are not prepared to accept the corollary, namely that *if the parents do not have faith, then there is no valid baptism*.

3

Infant Baptism –

the Atomised Sacrament
by
Colin Buchanan

Assistant Bishop in the
Diocese of Rochester

3

Infant Baptism – the Atomised Sacrament

The church in the New Testament practised a baptism of initiation which was fundamentally missionary. Enquirers were instructed to submit to baptism as submission to the gospel and were then reckoned to have been converted in the waters of baptism, and the gospel's claims on people's obedience were spread through this use of the sacrament.[1] Similarly at baptism the candidate was incorporated into a missionary fellowship; having confessed the faith of Christ for the first time at baptism, he or she was then expected to confess the same Jesus before the world thereafter.[2] The mission of God in which the candidate was now participant was exercised by a missionary *fellowship* into which the person was converted. In the fellowship the newcomer became a participant at the communal meals, and put his or her own home and goods at the disposal of the church. Infant baptism was practised, but it was a component of household baptisms, in which parents (and perhaps heads of extended families) brought their children and other dependants into the fellowship also, for them also to grow in faith and knowledge of Christ.[3] It is no part of my task here to argue a case for infant baptism, which I have endeavoured to do elsewhere, but only to point out that a minority community – whether in Jewish Jerusalem or pagan Philippi – needed to ensure that their children were fully participant with them in the sacramental and believing missionary fellowship.

Our problem today in the Church of England, and to a

lesser extent in the other fairly traditionalist Churches, is that baptism has in popular understanding lost its missionary and incorporative character, and has lodged in the folklore (and thus in the nation's subconscious) as a dollop of personal benefit which infants ought to receive after birth – just as fairly recently in England they used to receive free, state benefit, orange juice. It is the task of this essay to trace how popular belief over the centuries forgot the missionary role of baptism and almost lost its incorporative character also. This may help us to suggest ways of bringing both practice and rationale back to some approximation to the New Testament emphases.

Developments of the first millennium

In the pre-Nicene church, it looks as though this approach to baptism remained fairly constant. By the time of Hippolytus there was a lengthy catechumenate, finishing with a build-up through Lent to the night vigil, and baptisms at dawn on Easter morning. The new converts, whilst baptised in a private baptistery away from the assembly (perhaps because they were baptised naked), were then brought into the community, and were enabled to share the prayers, the kiss of peace (an important point of incorporation), and finally the eucharistic meal.[4] Persecution was still in the air, so that, quite apart from the rigours of the catechumenate, there was a great seriousness about the decision to undergo baptism, and thus to align oneself with this semi-underground religious society. So the sense of incorporation into that society was very strong at the baptism itself, and the only known way to *be* a Christian was through the gate of baptism into the context of that society.

Infants and children, we are told, were being baptised with the adults, and, whilst they may have been excused a three-year catechumenate, they too were in baptism becoming identified with the Christian community. It looks as though they too passed from the waters into the assembly, and concluded with the reception of communion, at however young an age.

The only early hint we have of a different approach is in Tertullian's famous deprecation of infant baptism. Here he seems to write solely of the moral responsibilities lying upon the baptised (and, by their sponsorship, upon the sponsors of infant candidates) – and the individual is considered alone (in a rather latterday way), without any sense of the sustaining power of the community, or of the context of a believing home, or of the eucharistic rhythm of the fellowship.[5] But then, if we read between the lines, we can perhaps detect that the infants and young children who are receiving baptism in Tertullian's account, against whose baptism he is protesting, are not from believing families at all. Some motivation, which we cannot easily penetrate, has led pagan parents to let their offspring be baptised. In the process, the weight of responsibility has passed from family and community to individual sponsors who often, being outside the family, cannot discharge their task effectively. Thus the incredibility of the particular rationale with which Tertullian is grappling (i.e. that the church can rely upon godparents to do a good job) has become self-evident. Tertullian then becomes an almost classic model for baptismal reformers today – his only mistake being that he has come to believe that all godparents or sponsors are morally answerable towards God for the behaviour of those whom they sponsor. He therefore rejects infant baptism because of that very rationale – as we would have to do also, if we could ground infant baptism nowhere but on that rationale. We differ in that we wish to *retain* infant baptism, rejecting Tertullian's rationale altogether, and pointing out that his account differs from the New Testament basis for infant baptism which we would rather advocate. From Tertullian's own account we must judge both that the rationale for infant baptism had changed, and that the practice had become distorted accordingly.[6]

If we go back to the Hippolytan account, there are some

elements of contrast with Tertullian: the 'responding' looks to
be more like 'articulating vows' which *truly belong to the
candidate* and are voiced by the proxy without the same moral
hostages given to fortune as in Tertullian; there is a primary
expectation that in fact parents are themselves bringing their
own infants (i.e. this is within Christian families); and the
infants are, we must presume, incorporated fully into the life
of the sacramental fellowship – for from then on they follow
the same route through baptism as their elders, being similarly greeted with the kiss of peace, being similarly incorporated
into the prayers, and being similarly apportioned a share in
the eucharistic bread and cup. It all looks much healthier than
in the Tertullian account.

However, the trends were to prove to be misleading. In the
fourth century Christianity came by stages to be first *licita*,
then favoured, then almost mandatory. Thousands flocked
into the church, and whilst many deferred their baptism – and
deferred it also for their children – in principle the flocking in
of first-generation adults spelled the future end of adult
initiation, and the corresponding growth in infant baptism.
This situation came to pass quite quickly as, in the years from
A.D. 400 to A.D. 600, the teaching of St Augustine (364–430)
bit deep into the Western church's practice. Augustine taught
that a child who dies unbaptised cannot catch the Beatific
Vision, but at best ends up in a nebulous limbo. Thus the
pressure was on – infant mortality rates were high, and
baptisms could not be saved up till Easter, could not be saved
till a bishop came by (or at least not in the large missionary
dioceses North of the Alps), and in the last analysis in the
Dark Ages and Middle Ages infants did not even have to be
saved up till the following Sunday when the parish priest
might give baptism in the context of the mass. No – the
pressures were so great so quickly upon birth that midwives
were learning that they could themselves administer a minimal baptism, and very generally did do so to the new-born.[7]
Thus incorporation into a 'missionary fellowship' was hardly
now the question – much more it was the individual dollop of

grace (or preservative) which was in view, and this was administered on an individualistic basis.

Not only were baptisms usually not done at the mass in the Middle Ages, but, whether they were or not, the reception of communion was generally not part of the rite. If the baptism was in church, the priest alone offered the mass, and he alone communicated. The people assisted – that is, they stood around. Whereas in Hippolytus' day the members bound themselves to each other by the prayers, the kiss, and the sharing one bread – and thus the newly baptised, adult or infant, belonged in the fellowship (cf. 1 Cor. 10:17) – now the baptism had become detached from the eucharist and incorporation was not visibly enacted. Finally, the cup was withdrawn from the laity from the thirteenth century onwards and, without the cup, infants could not be communicated at all, or at least not until weaned, which might be well into their second or even third year. And once this 'admission to communion' had been separated from baptism and come at an older age, then other pressures pushed the age up to 'first confession' at the age of seven. The eucharist itself in the Middle Ages did not look or feel like a fellowship meal, even at Easter when the general communion was ordered – but how much less did baptism speak of a fellowship. It was a private benefit, conveyed by a kind of tradesperson (though sometimes no doubt by the priest), with no clear corporate implications and no visible connection with eucharistic fellowship at all. If ever a rite were in line to become mumbo-jumbo – and, we insist, individualistic mumbo-jumbo – then that rite was infant baptism.

The universal character of medieval Western Christendom heightened this emphasis. To join a club of limited numbers – perhaps even a secret society, like Freemasonry – gives the entrance rite some significance as the initiate passes into the privileges and perhaps duties of membership. That is how baptism was, even for infants, in the ante-Nicene church. But to receive baptism simply because the whole country receives it at birth, as a standard post-natal ceremony, is to lose sight of its incorporating role. We may compare it with the receiving of an inoculation after birth today – the child does not thereby enter any club. That child has simply received the standard prescribed health-preserving dollop which, as an individual, he or she needs. So it was that infant baptism was experienced in the medieval West. It still had that element of being the background to the rest of life, but it was a very shadowy background, to which value largely got attached through the occasional rush to give it to a dying child. Its meaning to the living remained very much at the level of the sub-conscious – and what meaning it had was that of a preservative for the individual.

The reformation inheritance

The Reformers argued about infant baptism. But in the 'mainstream' churches – Anglican, Lutheran, or Reformed – they retained it, and retained it believing it to be not only inherited but justifiable from the scriptures. However, they were well caught in the medieval traps, for:

(a) they gave it to all children, and
(b) they argued its benefits largely in terms of the Lord's good-will towards the individual children, and
(c) they did nothing about restoring communion to baptised children, and therefore left the newly baptised still not admitted to communion – and indeed delayed admission to an older age than the medievalists had practised.[8]

The Reformed Churches deprecated 'private' baptisms of children in danger of death and instead ordered that children should be brought to church as quickly as possible. This was not only because they minded about the presence of the congregation, but also because they did not believe lay people should administer baptism. The minister held the power of the keys, and the responsibility for the administration of the sacraments, and he alone should preside at the rite. The Anglican Prayer Books from 1549 to 1662 reflect a tension between the medieval inheritance and the full Reformed principles on this very point, for private or 'clinical' baptism at home is still permitted, whilst the propriety of a lay administrant is disputed.[9]

On the other hand, the rationale as to *why* baptisms should be conducted in public was stated clearly – and yet was arguably also misleading. Baptisms were to come after the second lesson at Morning or Evening Prayer on Sundays, and were to be done so that *'the congregation . . . may testify the receiving of them that be newly baptized into the number of Christ's Church'* and also so that *'every man present may be put in remembrance of his own profession to God made in his baptism'*. Now, once private or 'clinical' baptism is acknowledged to *be* baptism, then a congregation cannot be indispensable for a baptism to be a baptism. So the rationale for baptism being public is bound to be slightly oblique or even cosmetic. Apparently the congregation are to be witnesses (i.e. they can 'testify') and to be personally stirred (i.e. they are to be 'put in remembrance'). But they do *not* seem to have any role in 'being the church' which receives the infant by baptism. They are not in fact there to be the body of Christ into which the person is received at baptism.[10] The strictly 'churchly' angle is missing from these baptisms – the stage is set, the people are to be there, but they are individuals and the church, *qua* church, is missing.

Clericalist centuries

To this it might be replied that the very role of the clergyman was to represent the church, even to 'be' the church to the parents and infant candidate. Representation is easy to understand as a principle, but when it is practised exhaustively it becomes something else – substitution. That is how medieval clericalism and sacerdotalism arose. It was purged of its more 'priestly' assumptions at the Reformation, but the ministerial usurpation of all churchly roles continued not only unabated, but with a fresh Protestant ideology to energise the inherited traditions. Thus, from the Reformation until within living memory, in virtually every parish in the land, admission to baptism, the preparation of the parents, and the arranging of the ritual event all lay entirely within the responsibility of the clergyman. If there were questions about the godparents (one of whom in the 1604 Canons was supposed to be a communicant), or about the name, or about the speed with which it could be arranged, or even (though this was rare till recently) as to whether the child should be baptised at all – then these questions lay entirely between parents and clergyman. There was no organ of 'the church' which could be invoked, or could express an interest – the issue was an arrangement between parents and clergyman for the benefit of the child: not unlike an arrangement made by parents with a bank-manager for the benefit of a child. Because the interviewing and arranging only involved these two parties, the concept of a corporate 'church', even if it was articulated in words, was never modelled in experience, and thus never took root in people's minds. It is astonishing that in many parishes this still continues – a clergy person (as we must now say) may have a high or a low doctrine of baptism, and a high or a low set of criteria for admitting the candidate to the sacrament – but as long as one individual alone wields the 'keys', so long will an individualised benefit to the candidate run strong in the tradition and the folklore. The outsider never meets the church in any corporate way, but only has to deal with the official who dispenses the benefit.

The current outcome

I need hardly stay on this point for its relevance today to stand out. Once the church is defined not as the whole nation (as in Henry VIII's day), nor even as all the baptised (as, say, in the first half of the present century), but essentially as those who actually meet, then the church has not only become more defined in its membership, but it is also changed in its role. It is now a church *with a mission* – a mission which logically begins with the fringe, and goes on to the baptised who are beyond the fringe, and finally to the whole nation. The candidate for baptism today is to be incorporated into a missionary church. He or she is to belong to a body, the members of which *love* one another and share a common role and purpose and sense of God's calling. *That*, I submit, cannot be explained by a ministerial interview or teaching session alone – it has to be 'felt' by encounter with the living worshipping church. The one-to-one interview between minister and parent, or the teaching session by a minister to a class of parents, cannot by definition convey the nature of the church. Thus ministers, even when talking about the church to enquiring parents, may actually connive by their own structure of interview at a wholly individualistic and static concept of what baptism means.

Other individualising

If this pattern of individualistic understanding is one which the church has willy-nilly conveyed to the world by its processes, there is another misconception with the same outcome at work within the church's own borders. This theological fifth column I sweepingly dub as 'Baptist'.[11] We shall see that it is not confined to Baptists, it does not always arise from Baptists, and certainly not all Baptists embrace it, but it is very typically Baptist, and it flows strongly from outside into Anglican congregations. To what do I refer? Why, to the teaching that baptism is a step in individual discipleship, to be undertaken as a personal response of obedience to Christ, at whatever point in life the inner conviction 'I ought to be baptised' comes to the individual believer. Because it is an individual response, many Baptist believers have gone all the way through adulthood without receiving it at all, and, in the most consistently individualistic circles, it would hardly be appropriate to urge another believer to receive baptism, as the church as such has no stakes in the individual's response except to confer baptism if asked. In many 'Open' Baptist circles neither participation in communion, nor church membership, nor even the holding of responsible office, has traditionally been confined to the baptised. Baptism as an individual testimony to what God has done in one's life, even though done in the presence of the church, has had little or no churchly reference.

Now it is my contention that at the evangelical end of the Church of England (and possibly at all sorts of other points on the spectrum) this 'Baptist' outlook has affected even Anglican understanding of the sacrament. Christians have come to the issue with a wholly individualistic question in their minds: 'What does baptism do for this or that person?' Often, no doubt, it has led to a flight from infant baptism, leading to either a tension within, or a parting from, Anglican churchmanship. But, even where infant baptism has been retained, it has been retained on an individualistic understanding – the rationale again becomes not what in baptism the church is doing, but what in baptism the individual gains. I was myself once curate in a parish where the answer to this latter question was clearly: 'the individual gains nothing and loses nothing, so the church can safely give it to all who ask without any awkwardness, and *without the issue touching at all upon our (wholly different) task of preaching the gospel*'! But my point is equally valid if a parish concludes that, in particular cases, as the individuals gain nothing, and are possibly inoculated against the gospel, baptism should *not* be administered. It does not matter which of these two opposite results emerges, nor even which in the economy of God is 'right' or 'wrong'; if it emerges on the basis of questions confined to the individual, then even the 'right' result runs the risk of doing theological evil that good may come.

Evangelicals in the Church of England have had around a

century and a half of semi-conscious anti-sacramentalism. Ever since the days of Pusey and Philpotts, they have feared the teaching that men and women receive grace virtually in proportion to their frequency in receiving sacraments. The more they have been driven into a minority complex, the more they have been moulded by these outside forces into a distorted shape, awry from their biblical birthright. Their context has not helped them – conniving until the 1960s in the baptism of all infants born in the land, they have known in experience that the gospel of conversion had nothing to do with the practice of baptism! It has been important to deny that 'baptism makes you a Christian'. Equally, holding a very lightweight doctrine of the visible church, they have been unable to give any ecclesial significance to baptism; and working in undenominational ways to preach an individualistic gospel (as especially exemplified in the great evangelistic campaigns from Moody to Billy Graham), they have been unable also to give much churchly significance to conversion. To be baptised, to be converted, and to 'join a church' have not only been three separate activities, which in the New Testament are one – they have also been three separate activities without any logical links between them. No wonder then that the anti-sacramentalists were as often to be found in indiscriminate practices as were the super-sacramentalists – not because such practices were connected to a wrong doctrine of the church, but because they were connected to no Christian doctrine whatsoever.

The discovery of a conscience about which infants are proper candidates for baptism can be particularly documented over the last three decades. In part the Parish and People movement of the 1950s gave the lead. Ernie Southcott at Halton brought baptisms into the Parish Communion, and took strong steps to incorporate parents and children into the active life of the church. The leaders of the movement stood away from the legal establishment of religion and cried: 'Let the church be the church'. There is little evidence that they went further and attempted to give realistic baptismal boundaries to the church, but they certainly affected the atmosphere.[12]

A further stage had to come. A policy which takes infant baptism as both a gospel sacrament and a churchly sacrament must provide for the serious possibility (whether by parental withdrawal or churchly refusal) of any infant *not* being baptised. The first well-documented policies were to be found in the 1960s amongst evangelicals, and their rise must be related to the concerns expressed by evangelicals at the Keele Congress in 1967 that they should have a high doctrine of the visible church, a positive valuing of sacraments (including a good conscience biblically about the *principle* of baptising infants), and a full-orbed internally consistent pastoral ministry.[13] It is not the part of this essay to trace the slow recovery of a doctrine of the church by evangelicals – and there is still a long way to go – but that is the head of steam which produced movement on the baptismal front. That is not to say that others were not getting there also, and since the 1960s there have been ever-growing signs of the unease in the church on the issue of indiscriminate baptism.[14]

Transition to mission

It is clear that this growing unease of clergy and laity has related to the steady secularisation of English society over the last three decades. It has become more and more clear that many families seeking baptism are not even minimally Christian, and the conscience of the church has grown accordingly. It has simultaneously taken aboard 'mission' as a priority in England, whereas in 1960 it is doubtful if more than a handful saw 'mission' as meaning other than evangelism in Africa.

However, both the folklore and the establishment problems remain. As long as the folklore teaches that 'the child will never do well till it's christened' so long will the demand be there (though this is, of course, now dying slowly of attrition).[15] The 'establishment' factor then comes into play:

if there is any reason to think that parishioners have by sheer birth a part and stake under the law in their local Anglican parish church, so long will an untheological or opportunist clergy prefer to bend to the folklore, rather than engage their congregation in modelling the loving missionary fellowship to the enquirers. For the establishment itself has become the thickest of fogs to obscure the mission of the church. If all the baptised are vaguely members of the church, or putatively born again, then there are no boundaries to the fellowship, and no grounds for being even cautious about a 'child's right to baptism'. Where establishment rules, ecclesiality departs. Where there are no boundaries, there is no one outside them – and no meaning to being inside either. But if God has set his church on earth, as a gathered company with a true mission to the world, then for the gospel's sake we must bury the establishment and let infant baptism be seen in its true missionary and corporate perspective.[16]

And then there is the positive side to the sharpening of the issues. Children are to be baptised in believing families, and then be brought up in an admittedly minority cult to share with their parents in this unpopular faith. The smaller the minority, the higher the gospel profile – and the more sure it is that the church will be wholeheartedly missionary. It is to *that* that the baptismally incorporated children of believing homes will be brought up. It is a most demanding task for parents in a secularised or religiously indifferentist atmosphere. But that is what infant baptism is about.

4

Grasping the Nettle

Baptismal Reform in the Church of England since 1940
by
Clifford Owen

Rector of Clifton upon Teme,
Lower Sapey
and the Shelsleys
(*Diocese of Worcester*)

4

Grasping the Nettle

Baptismal Reform in the Church of England since 1940

In June 1985 I wrote a letter to the *Church of England Newspaper*. It was about infant baptism. I wrote it in response to a feature article that had appeared two weeks previously about the report published shortly after the second world war entitled *Towards the Conversion of England*. The point I made in my letter was that there was one simple step which could do more to further evangelism than anything else: the reform of the popular practice of infant baptism, especially through canon law. In particular I argued that Anglican priests should have the right to refuse baptism where it was clearly pastorally inappropriate. Especially this applied where the parents of infants brought to baptism had virtually no tangible connections with the worshipping life of the church.

From the correspondence that followed it was obvious that there is still a deep division of opinion in this matter. Some letters gave unquestioned support to what I proposed; others saw any move to tighten up the 'open' policy of the Church of England as a restriction upon the grace of God.

Over the years there has been no lack of clergy who have voiced concern over the matter of baptising all and sundry. Philip Crowe, for example, speaks for most of these when he says: 'The service creates the illusion that the children belong to God in his church when in fact they do not. Plainly, to baptise babies who are not the children of Christian parents is a most damaging abuse of Christian baptism.'[1] But where extreme reluctance is found is in the will to effect change on a church-wide scale. This, I would maintain, is the nettle that must be grasped, if baptism is to have anything like its New Testament significance, namely . . . a response to the gospel.

In this essay I want to trace the line of debate about baptism reform in the Church of England since 1940, to show the continuity of concern over the issue, and to argue that the time has now come for the Church of England to commit itself publicly to a policy of discriminate infant baptism.

It would seem nonsense, given the social and religious conditions of England at the close of the twentieth century, to profess concern for evangelism and not to face the inseparable issue of baptismal discipline. Bridge and Phypers in their excellent summary book *The Water that Divides*[2] have charted the parallel paths of infant baptism and believers' baptism down through the centuries. Their work points to one inescapable conclusion: the baptismal debate is a smouldering fire that refuses to go out and periodically flares up into prominence.

Within this debate two main rivers of controversy need to be distinguished. The first is the main infant/believers' baptism divide; and the second is the discriminate/indiscriminate debate within infant baptism. Now the Church of England has made provision for adult baptism since 1662 and adults are frequently baptised. It is the divide between discriminate and indiscriminate infant baptism which is the main issue of debate in this essay. If the Church of England were to take its stand on the opposite bank of this river, it might well find itself in a new country.

Before proceeding it is worth mentioning two notable and relevant protests near the turn of the century. Hensley Henson, who was to become Bishop of Hereford and later Durham, used a university sermon at Oxford in 1896 when he was vicar of Barking to condemn the modern practice of infant baptism as 'indecent in itself, discreditable to the church, and highly injurious to religion'. In 1907 Roland Allen resigned as vicar of Chalfont St Peter, principally over infant baptism. He saw that Anglican baptismal policy made no attempt to distinguish between those members of the church who thought that as believers they had obligations, and those who felt that they had a right to belong regardless. These two, Henson and Allen, found that the stone rocked, but could not move it from the entrance to the tomb.[3]

The modern baptismal debate: Alec Vidler

But it is an article published in July 1940, just ten weeks before the Battle of Britain, that appears to mark the start of the modern baptismal debate. It appeared in *Theology* and was written by the then editor, Alec Vidler. It was provocatively entitled 'Baptismal Disgrace'.[4] Vidler begins by noting the general malaise into which the subject of baptism had sunk. In the theological section of a certain library he noted just twenty books on baptism, only two of which had been published this century, and none since 1925. He asks: 'Is then the neglect of the subject to be accounted for by an unavowed and maybe unconscious fear of the embarrassing consequences that would ensue upon a close attention to it? Is it because the elucidation of theological principle with regard to our existing baptismal practice would impel us to disturbing and unpopular action that we have found it easy to pass by on the other side?'

The significance of Vidler's opening questions has not lessened in fifty years. When I first questioned some other clergy on the matter of baptismal discipline and the direction in which they felt reform should go, I discovered that concern was widespread but I also found a real reluctance to initiate any significant change. After a chapter meeting at which I had introduced the subject of baptismal discipline as a main item on the agenda, an older clergyman who had said nothing in the meeting came up to me and said: 'You know, I think it [infant baptism] ought to have been done away with years ago'.

When I was an ordinand I had my eldest son baptised in the chapel of my theological college in the main communion service. The principal said on the occasion: 'We are about to baptise a baby, and I know some of you must be wondering why!' Indeed I remember the general atmosphere of unbelief in the college chapel that morning which seemed to emanate from my fellow ordinands. I wonder in retrospect how many of my fellow ordinands of just fifteen years ago will be in fifteen years' time rather like the older clergyman after that chapter meeting, seasoned practitioners of infant baptism, surviving the course with a barely satisfying theology, perhaps sensing the need for reform but reluctant to seek it or even express it. I believe there must be many such clergy in parochial ministry today, and they may well have been around for generations. Probably these men more than any others hold the key to baptismal reform.

Vidler notes that he was encouraged to discover: 'that among the younger clergy there are some – perhaps *many* [my italics] – who are determined to think this matter out and, so far as it lies within their power, to bring practice into line with principle'. In other words what is theologically wrong cannot be pastorally right. From the comparative safety of his position as editor of *Theology* he was bold to admit that when he had been himself in a parish his conscience had been uneasy on the matter.

Vidler goes on to consider the question of the theological basis for baptising infants. For him infant baptism is the doorway to the church '(a momentous occasion in a man's life), the church which is *socially distinct* [my italics] from the world, which makes demands, and secures to him blessings.' His basis for infant baptism is primarily 'household baptism'. He urges strongly that only the infants of believing parents should be baptised. I note that the term 'indiscriminate' is already in use in Vidler's essay. Indeed, its origin in connection with infant baptism is credited to Hensley Henson.

Vidler then speculates from where reform might come. The best source, and the most effective, would be the hierarchy, but he adds that the bishops are very busy men and after all who would want to stretch his agenda by including a hornets' nest! But, inevitably, it is in the direction of the 'inferior clergy' that he looks and indeed below their ranks to the then 'unemancipated laity' for a lead in the matter. Before leaving Vidler, we ought to note that he does not blame the non-Christian parents who requested baptism for the present state of affairs, but he lays the blame at the door of the whole church and not least the clergy themselves.

1940–1965: *Status quo* on radical reform . . .

Vidler's plea was powerful (I am tempted to use the word 'prophetic') for it heralded and foreshadowed the initiation debate of the last forty years. The fork which he pushed into the garden of initiation loosened the soil, but did not begin to remove the weeds.

Not unexpectedly Vidler's essay drew immediate responses. Two letters were printed in the August 1940 edition of *Theology*. One was written by a parochial clergyman in the Church of Scotland (Revd. D. B. MacGregor) who rebutted Dr. Vidler's position from an automatic efficacy (*ex opere operato*) position. The infant was made a member of Christ by grace in baptism independently of any faith on the parents' part. The correspondent went on to lament that in Scotland, baptism of infants was not indiscriminate enough!

The second letter was written by John Moorman, who gave an unqualified welcome to Vidler's article.[5] Indeed we can sense a sigh of relief behind Moorman's response. He contrasted first the way in which the two gospel sacraments were conducted: The first, holy communion, was attended by much dignity and reverence; the other, holy baptism, was often performed in an atmosphere which was charged with hypocrisy and superstition. He laments the difficulties in inducing the clergy to see how unsatisfactory was the present system of indiscriminate baptism. When he pleaded at a chapter meeting for a discussion given the *urgency* (italics mine) of the problem, he was told that they had 'done all that'. Moorman suggests three improvements:

1. Baptisms only once a month and instruction for the sponsors
2. If a family have children over five years of age not yet attending Sunday school then the baptism of further children in that family should be delayed until the over fives have joined the Sunday school
3. Efforts should be made to ensure that at least one godparent is a practising member of the church.

These suggestions have a dated feel to them now, but it is sobering to realise that fifty years ago reforms were being specified in these practical terms. Finally Moorman suggested that no such reforms would be effective unless the clergy acted *corporately* (italics mine).

The two letters from MacGregor and Moorman were doubtless sifted from a large pile, and chosen to represent the two poles of the discriminate/indiscriminate divide. But the modern debate was opened and it has remained open.

The Revd. Cyril Pocknee, chairman of the Baptism Reform Movement, writing in the preface to his book *The Rites of Christian Initiation*,[6] said that in the 'last two decades pastoral problems relating to the administration of Holy Baptism have been the subject of frequent discussion . . . we now realise that our pastoral problems cannot be resolved, neither can there be any satisfactory revision of the rites of baptism and confirmation in the Book of Common Prayer, until a number of theological issues relating to the rites of initiation have been clarified.'[7]

Some of these earlier concerns about indiscriminate infant baptism led a few parishes to adopt discriminate baptism

policies, and this caused much controversy. The debate
turned to whether the Anglican position squared with New
Testament theology; it centred on the question of the inter-
relation of baptism with confirmation. Following the report,
Confirmation Today (1944), opinion was sought by Convocation from deaneries on experience in the parish with baptism
and confirmation preparation. Welsby records the conclusion
of this investigation: 'That no far reaching change was desired
by the majority of the clergy in the traditional patterns
of initiation'.[8]

However, the 1954 report prepared for the Convocations of
Canterbury and York entitled *Baptism and Confirmation
Today*,[9] revealed the divergence of thinking on baptismal
discipline among members of the commission. Three members of the Canterbury Convocation committee (out of a total
of seventeen) issued a subsequent minority report. An
explanatory note in the main report states that the three:
'have indicated at least two main differences from the view of
the majority of the members. They view with grave disquiet
the present discipline of infant baptism, which in their opinion
cannot be justified and is *in need of radical alteration* [italics
mine], and in connection with the theology of baptism and
confirmation their view is much nearer to the Mason–Dix
view than to the traditional view accepted by most members
of the Joint Committee.'[10]

Dr. Beasley-Murray in his foreword to *Baptism Today and
Tomorrow*,[11] noted that for the first part of this century
discussion on baptism had largely been the preserve of theologians, but was now passing into the ministerial ranks and
even to the laity. He cited a *Church of England Newspaper*
poll taken early in 1965 on whether changes in the administration of baptism ought to be initiated in the Church of England. An unexpected feature was the high proportion of lay
members of the church (of both sexes) who wished to see
radical reform. This suggested that the reformist lobby was
growing. But had a similar poll been taken by the *Church
Times*, the results might have been otherwise as the *C.E.N.*

and the *C.T.* twenty years ago were much more inclined to be 'party' newspapers.

The 1965 Ecumenical Conference

Again we see the pattern of a minority in favour of radical reform at the 1965 Ecumenical Conference at Swanwick sponsored by the Parish and People movement.[12] The conference was split into four commissions each focusing on a different aspect of baptism. They were:

1. preparation for initiation
2. restitution of the lapsed
3. the liturgical setting of initiation
4. indiscriminate baptism

In the fourth commission various votes were taken. The commission had sixty-one people of whom five were non-Anglicans. They were asked to state their preference for:

1. continuing with present Church of England practice
2. restricting infant baptism to children of committed Christians
3. moving to believers' baptism only, with a blessing ceremony for infants

At a first vote proposals 2. and 3. were combined and the results were as follows:

	Whole Commission	*Anglicans*
Proposal 1.	6	6
Proposal 2. or 3.	52	47
Those abstaining from voting	3	3

The 52 members who voted for proposal 2. or 3. were then asked to vote again in favour of either 2. or 3., with the following result:

	Whole Commission	*Anglicans*
Proposal 2.	26	21
Proposal 3.	23	23
Those abstaining from voting	3	3

These figures at first sight would suggest an overwhelming vote in favour of baptismal reform in the Church of England. However when a reframed motion was put to the debate of the whole conference a much more divided picture emerged. The full motion urged the following reforms:

1. The church should exhibit more clearly by its corporate life the fruits of baptism [in fact a call for spiritual renewal].
2. The church should adopt new rites of baptism to show the meaning of the sacrament in more contemporary terms.
3. The teaching of the church about baptism should be redefined and made public in such ways that the meaning and implications of the sacrament are more readily understood.
4. The baptism of those able to answer for themselves should be the norm.[13] Where the practice of infant baptism is continued it should be limited to families where there is good evidence of Christian commitment . . . the church should devise standards of pastoral practice similar to those in other lands applicable to both infant and adult baptism. We wish to see the baptism of those able to answer for themselves made much more visible as the theological and pastoral standard of Christian initiation [abbreviated].[14]
5. Appropriate forms of service [are] to be used where an infant is not baptised.
6. Wherever possible these proposals should be examined and acted upon on an ecumenical basis.

The debate was extremely tense, and indicated how deeply the conference felt about the issue. As expected, the first three resolutions were adopted decisively (98 per cent majority) and motion 6. was carried unanimously. However items 4. and 5. were hotly debated and eventually a proposal was made that these two items be not put to the vote. The reason for so doing was because unlike members of the commission on indiscriminate baptism, the rest of the conference had had insufficient time to consider the matter. The items were not in fact put to the vote and thus the conference stepped back from what could have been a very influential vote for baptismal reform in the Church of England. But at least the real issues were beginning to emerge from the shadows.

The *Ely Report*, 1971

What then can we make of the *Ely Report* of 1971?[15] Its main recommendation was that baptism should become the complete and full initiatory rite of the church with a laying on of hands. This would be followed by early admission to communion. Traditional confirmation would then come later as a 'commissioning'. The report was sifted into a working paper by the Revd. Peter Cornwell.[16]

The Bishop of Ely, in introducing the report to Synod, pressed for an early decision. In the ensuing debates, the main recommendation of the report was not carried. It would have entailed a radical change in the Church of England's pattern of initiation – a major break with its Catholic past. The Revd. Peter Jagger noted that several other churches in the Anglican Communion had faced the same initiation issues as the Church of England, but had come to different conclusions. He urged that 'whenever radical changes are suggested their premises, logic, and objections must be carefully examined'.[17] This was primarily in response to the Bishop of Ely's request for haste. The real problem, Jagger noted, was the disintegration of the complete rite in the early centuries. The Doctrinal Commission of the Church in Wales concluded in 1971:

> Any separation of baptism, confirmation and first communion either as successively given at different stages in the initiation rite, or as conceivable in isolation from one another, involves grave theological confusion. This is why the disintegrated pattern of Christian Initiation, which the Western Church has inherited,

is theologically unsatisfactory. Such separation leads to pseudo-problems that are insoluble theologically, if not in fact meaningless.[18]

But this takes us slightly off track. Did the *Ely Report* take up the problem of discipline in infant baptism, especially in the direction suggested by the 1965 Ecumenical Conference? My personal opinion was that it did; but only to the water's edge without crossing the river. The Cornwell document (see note 16 above) contained the following paragraph:

> The church has to decide whether infant baptism should be administered to the children of parents who not only make the promises, but also show evidence that they will fulfil them, or whether infant baptism should continue to be the request of the parents, with the sole condition that they should make the promises. To decide for the former would involve a change in church law. To decide for the latter would be to work within the framework of existing law.[19]

This surely is the nub of the matter and the main decision that the Church of England must face. It was the point that I made in my letter to the *Church of England Newspaper* (see opening paragraph of essay). If baptismal discipline is to be reformed then it can only be effected in the longer term via canon law. The General Synod of fifteen years ago had a chance to make that decision. In the event the Synod veered towards the second option. The essential part of the motion finally passed read: ' that infant baptism should continue to be available to the children of all parents that request it and are willing and able to make the requisite promises'. The words 'and able' were a successful amendment by Christopher Wansey who nudged the motion away from the indiscriminate direction it was taking.

Colin Buchanan, who had unsuccessfully moved a motion for Synod to take the discriminate view, noted that whilst the addition of the clause 'and able' had been welcome it might be interpreted as meaning no more than 'having the power of speech'.[20]

Thus the position of Synod in this matter and consequently the authorised discipline within the Church of England was rather anomalous and bi-focal. Synod did not sanction discriminate baptism. It wanted positive baptismal teaching, and yet it winked at a broad spectrum of baptismal practice in the parishes.

However, Series 2 baptism service made clearer demands. In the preface to the rite of infant baptism a Christian upbringing is spelt out in terms of teaching, public worship and the prayers and example of parents and sponsors. Colin Buchanan infers from this preface that canon law has shifted its ground to a more selective and demanding baptismal policy. The shift, he says, raises numerous problems not yet faced by the Church of England. Because the General Synod resolution 'appeared to be somewhat fudged', parishes, deaneries, and dioceses are free to make their own policy decisions.[21] This is roughly how we find the present situation across the church.

The main *Ely Report* had recommended that baptism should be offered to all who 'sincerely desired' it, and suggested that a good test of sincere desire was the readiness of the parents to receive instruction to help them take a sincere part in the rite of baptism.[22] This, on the face of it, gives parishes a degree of flexibility. And it is to the parish that we must now direct our attention. Although there has been no major debate on initiation in Synod since *Ely*, the last fifteen years have been a period of experiment in the matter of baptism preparation and discipline.

It would seem that 'parish policy' is now the key phrase in understanding baptismal discipline. These days most incumbents do not think in terms of a universal Anglican baptismal policy, but see the adopting of a local policy as part of general pastoral duty. At a rural deans' meeting with one diocesan bishop in 1984, baptismal discipline was one point on the agenda. The inference, according to the minutes of the meeting, was that there was a divergence of policy among the parishes of the diocese; but the important issue was that clergy should respect the practice of other clergy across a deanery. Some rural deans felt that there was a need for guidelines (from whom was not discussed). This was felt to be particularly important where a 'strict' parish and an 'open' one were in close proximity.[23]

What is the range of baptismal policies today?

An attempt to categorise the range of baptismal policies that can be found across the church has been made in the table and diagram that follow. Doubtless there are many refinements and variations on the six categories suggested, but it seems to me that they reflect fairly both sides of the indiscriminate/discriminate divide. Category 6 which I have labelled the 'red zone', represents a position of baptising only those who are able to answer for themselves. This is almost certainly the rarest situation but it has been tried (Christopher Wansey made a bold experiment at Roydon in the matter).[24] Categories 4 and 5 represent parishes where definite evidence of Christian commitment is required of at least one parent before baptism of an infant is undertaken. Both of these categories represent a clear discriminatory practice.

AN ATTEMPT TO CLASSIFY BAPTISMAL POLICIES IN THE PARISHES

1 'all comers'   An open policy. Accepted by many as the traditional position of the Church of England.

Baptism is never refused or delayed to

any who request it. Minimal canonical conditions met e.g. all sponsors baptised but need not be confirmed. Normal preparation is by clergyman on first contact. 'Bookings' made at first contact. Parents are unlikely to be communicants or in regular worship. Subsequent children are baptised even if little response shown after the baptism of first child.

2 as 1 but with preparation

Open policy with preparation: All are baptised who request it but preparation may involve a group, a course, or some attendance at worship.

3 'hurdles' policy

As for 2 but the course is tougher and may be longer. A date for the baptism may not be given until some parts of the preparation are completed.

The alternative service of thanksgiving for the birth of a child may be strongly urged on families where there is no desire for commitment.

Where parents are co-habiting some assurance of the intention to consider Christian marriage may be sought before proceeding with the baptism.

4 communicant status

Practising communicant status required of one parent before baptism of infant agreed to. Based on the principle that the baptismal promises cannot be made on behalf of another if the parent has not taken them first upon him/herself.

Lapsed communicants are encouraged to return to the fold.

Theological basis: covenant theology.

5 rigorist

Only children of established church families who have been worshipping in the church well prior to the baptism of their child. Clear evidence of Christian faith and life sought from enquirers, or at very least from one parent.

6 only those able to answer for themselves

'Red zone!': A few parishes will only baptise those who are able to answer for themselves. This may include young children where appropriate. Canon B22 is cited as a 'conscience clause' for clergy not wishing to carry out baptisms of those who cannot answer for themselves.

Categories 1., 2. and 3. probably account for the greater part of Church of England parishes. I must point out again that the divide between 3. and 4. is probably wider and deeper than we think. However intense the baptismal instruction and preparation, it still results in quite large numbers of infants baptised with parents having little intention of any regular commitment to a local congregation. It really means that the local church is prepared to baptise those who come to it from outside in full recognition of the possibility that its highest hopes for a family may not be realised. This is the 'sincere desire' of the *Ely Report*; the willingness to receive instruction. The most careful pastoral preparation and follow-up by clergy and people cannot guarantee that parents requesting baptism will commit themselves to church membership. But there is no doubt that some parishes testify to good fruit in this area. However, if arguments are needed from statistics for baptismal reform then we only need refer to the 27,000,000 baptised in Great Britain, of whom only 6,000,000 have been confirmed and only 1,300,000 are Easter communicants (1986). The believers' only baptist would retort the obvious and suggest that it is the institution of infant baptism itself which is at fault. But the thoroughgoing 'infant baptist' surely

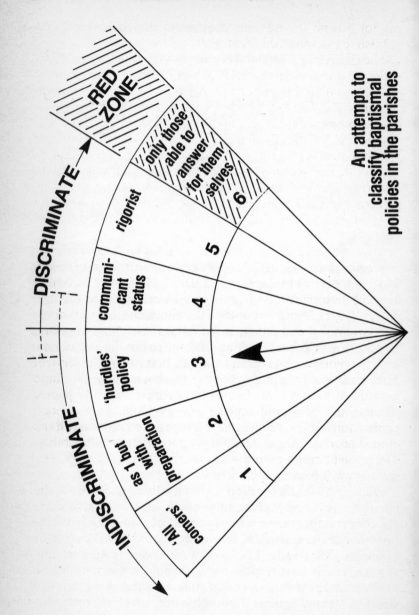

An attempt to classify baptismal policies in the parishes

RED ZONE

DISCRIMINATE

INDISCRIMINATE

'All comers'

as 1 but with preparation

'hurdles' policy

communi-cant status

rigorist

only those able to answer for themselves

1 2 3 4 5 6

cannot escape the obvious conclusion that it is our infant baptismal discipline that is at fault.

The *Church of England Newspaper* has in the last two years reported on several parishes where stricter policies have yielded increased membership. Michael Botting in his book *Teaching the Families* writes: 'I have discovered from personal experience that there are real gains from a strict baptismal policy'.[25] Colin Buchanan referring to Michael Botting's parish writes: 'a pattern of instruction and worship was set up which directed parents towards professing their own faith at confirmation, and then being regular communicants. This in turn qualified their children for baptism.' He went on to say that a steady trickle of adults was converted by this means.[26]

My experience of involvement with implementing stricter baptismal policies is mainly confined to moving from category 1 to 3 (see above) in stages over a period of ten years. Coming as a curate to a new housing area I quickly learned that the parish had traditionally baptised all who requested it. Parents were encouraged to choose baptised and confirmed sponsors, and there was at very least an attempt to familiarise parents with the requirements of baptism and their part in the service. The traditional vicar's visit to the home was the time honoured method of baptismal preparation. A glance through the baptismal register revealed that only a small proportion of parents had made any regular contact with the church even at festivals and allowing for high social mobility. The usual attempts at follow up: visiting, Sunday School, etc. were made but with only token success.[27]

Starting from this position my rector (who had been in the parish for two years before I joined the team) began to share his concern that our baptism procedures needed to be reviewed. We gave hours of time over several years to looking at the problem. Such discussions were always in earnest, and the amount of time consumed betrayed our concern that so much pastoral time and energy was invested in a large and steadily moving group of people whose spiritual route by-

passed the mainstream life of the congregation. Our discussions nearly always exposed the classic tension between
the desire to do sincere pastoral work on the one hand, and
the feeling that we might well be diminishing a gospel sacrament in the process, on the other. This is familiar territory to
many Anglican parish clergy. We made attempts to find out
what people really wanted in infant baptism; we encouraged
them to articulate their feelings in preparation groups. These
groups were useful as pastoral encounters but not much fruit
issued in the shape of increased membership. It had become
obvious that (as a result of decades of experience of sections
of the community with the occasional offices, particularly the
more rural close-knit communities) baptism was nearly
always a social occasion surrounded with superstition. It
was hardly ever linked in the mind with any deeper, congre-
gational commitment. We discovered, as many other clergy
have over the years, that most people requesting baptism for
their offspring, are quite unmoved by our best efforts to
educate them theologically.

What ways are there out of this impasse?

One way is to take 'folk religion' seriously. In his penetrating
study of ministry in the occasional offices Wesley Carr accepts
the givenness of the Anglican parish expectation, and seeks to
analyse the reality of the pastoral encounter.[28] He assumes a
very high level of theological and pastoral skill in the interviewing minister, and expects him to initiate a genuine dialogue with the requester of baptism in which, starting from
the language forms of the requester, he or she (usually she) is
slowly initiated into Christian concepts. I wonder how many
of us have the skills (or the time) to work through a dialogue
to the point where a freely made change is initiated in
someone requesting baptism, presumably towards a more
serious enquiry into the gospel. By God's grace it happens
and has happened several times, but these are the exceptions

in my experience, and not the rule. Carr makes an important point for all who would initiate change in baptismal discipline: 'One thing is sure. If for centuries the church has insisted on the baptism of infants, actively persuaded parents to have it done, and urged it as a duty to God, and to the child, it is not possible to reverse that teaching by a mere change of doctrinal stance'.[29] With Vidler, Carr would not lay the 'blame' for our baptismal difficulties upon the shoulders of those who would request it. He sees the minister as not simply representing himself and his own theological convictions, but as representing the whole institution. Enquirers bring institutional expectations with them. They feel offended when these expectations are not met by a priest whose personal convictions are at variance with these expectations. As a consolation, Carr gratefully tackles the question of how the minister can handle the tension which he finds generated in these encounters! However, he accepts the institution of infant baptism and does not discuss the possibility that the institution itself might be in need of reform.

In our parish staff discussions we found that 'folk religion' did not provide a satisfying resting place. If we granted that people had genuine religious needs at points in the life cycle, was it right to allow a gospel sacrament to be used as a vehicle for such needs to be expressed, especially if there was a theological chasm between the perceived need and our understanding of Christian baptism?

The provision in *The Alternative Service Book* of the 'Thanksgiving for the birth of a child' is a legitimate and convenient alternative for a parish to use for many families who would normally request infant baptism, but again it is not widely taken up. Some parishes are experimenting with a policy of insisting upon it as a first step towards baptism. We need to measure the effects of this over a longer term. It seems a good first foray into the realm of providing a rite which more accurately expresses the spiritual and emotional feelings associated with a baby's birth.

The second main way out of the impasse is to restore the

sacrament of baptism with its true meaning of initiation into
Christ. Baptism should be (as Vidler said) a momentous
occasion in a man's life. It should mark a deep spiritual
crossing point, but does it? Initiation for the evangelists is
marked by such responses as 'getting up out of one's seat',
signing a decision card, raising a hand. All of these are
baptism substitutes if they really signify Christian decision.
But can anything be a substitute for baptism? Most Anglican
clergy are agreed that baptism requests present the great
opportunity for teaching the gospel; but is it possible in the
pastoral encounter to put baptism to one side in order to
discuss the nature of the gospel? This seems to me to be a
basic pastoral requirement if a minister is to have some
freedom to manoeuvre. Creating this 'space' in order to
present the gospel and invite a response is essential if baptism
is to be restored to anything like its proper place.

The canons are behind us here in that they accept the need
to delay baptism if necessary in the interests of instruction
(Canon B22.4) but again the gospel is never a matter of mere
instruction. The dilemma principally arises when people press
for baptism whilst wanting to reject the gospel. Here a priest
may salve his conscience a little if he holds a reductionist view
of baptism (or at least of infant baptism). If it is a symbol
rather than a sacrament, signifying but not effecting, then it
might not appear to matter too much if we find ourselves
having to administer it to some of whom we are doubtful.
However, I do not believe we have a mandate in the New
Testament to use baptism as a 'wet visual aid'.[30] Those who
justify infant baptism as a proclamation of prevenient grace
seem to come close to this. It is the preaching of the gospel
which converts. The sacrament is then our response.

I have spelt this out at length, because whether we lean
towards an accommodation to folk religion, or to a higher
doctrine of baptism,[31] there are some pretty fierce tensions
likely to build up in any minister who takes his responsibilities
with any seriousness.

Most probably fear that to attempt to carry out a discriminate baptism policy[32] will invite hostility from the parish and little support from those in higher authority. The more able and confident will be found functioning effectively in any context. Colin Buchanan says that 'law is the way of the coward'. I find this a strange statement. It really ducks the issue, as a change in baptism law and discipline would effect the greatest single change in the Church of England's approach. For the majority of clergy there is, I believe, a clear need to take further steps in the reform of baptismal discipline. What ought those steps to be?

I believe there should be two. The first is the formal approval of discriminate infant baptism as a normal pastoral practice.[33] Second, in order to effect this, clergy should be granted the right of discretion to accept or delay individual baptisms. As and when these two steps are taken the church needs to state publicly its policy.

There is nothing new in the first proposal. It was embodied in the full motion of the 1965 Swanwick Ecumenical Conference (see above). It was faced as a possible option in the Synod debates after the Ely Report. Policies of this sort already operate in many parishes and it is arguable that they do so within the terms of the existing canons, rubrics, and the Synod motion passed in the Seventies. Whilst it was recognised that the phrase 'willing and able to make the promises' could mean no more than 'having the power of speech', it could by a similar token be argued that parents who show no evidence of Christian faith or life are not able to make the promises. For as long as this somewhat anomalous position pertains, it is by no means clear where the church stands especially in the eyes of the public. What is now needed is a clear provision for parishes to practise discriminate baptisms. There will no doubt be many parishes who will be happy to continue with more open policies, but it will be better if the General Synod makes a positive statement expressing the mind of the church. Once the local clergyman has discretion to accept or delay a baptism, then the way is clear for the nettle to be grasped parish by parish. Free Church ministers already have this discretion. When I recently questioned one of them how he viewed having this authority he replied that it was in the intrinsic nature of being a minister of Word and Sacrament. When I enquired further if he had ever used his authority to refuse baptism (particularly of an infant) he replied 'no'. Giving the same discretion to an Anglican minister would not necessarily lead to a rapid 'fencing of the font', but it is important that this authority be given. Granted that in an episcopal church the cure of souls is 'mine and thine' the weight of decision ought to lie with the man who is pastorally closer to the candidate (or his parents).

Delegating discretion is also important pastorally for the creation of 'space' as mentioned above. When those approaching the church for the baptism of their offspring are aware that it is not a *fait accompli*, they will be much more open to the gospel. After all, what is our goal in the matter? It is worth noting the words of Colin Buchanan in this context:[34]

> Goals are easier to state than achieve. And the goal in relation to infant baptism is as yet only half-stated. For ultimately a baptismal policy must not be that of any one parish or congregation, it must be that of the whole church of God. There must be a solidarity of practice across the whole face of the church. Parents must know that wherever they go, the same demands of practising membership will be made of them.

In saying this Colin Buchanan has stated the goal. If we delegate discretion to local clergy, I am saying that this step more than any other would be likely to achieve this goal. Of course I would want to state that at the parish level the baptismal policy should ideally be worked out within the ministerial team and with the P.C.C. But I believe that it is imperative that the whole church takes to itself its responsibility for the right administration of the sacrament of initiation. This must include saying 'no' where baptism is pastorally inappropriate. There are bound to be some initial difficulties, particularly from the public.

Peter Jagger writes: 'The practice of confining Christian initiation to the children of Christian parents would not at first be well received by those outside the "fellowship of the church".[35] It would however be a return to the primitive situation and practice, not out of any antiquarian idealism but through theological honesty as to what it really means to belong to the church'.

The revision of canon law relating to baptism, and the reformulating of the Synod motion passed in the *Ely Report* debates are two of the essential legislative tasks which would need to accompany the reforms I am advocating. Neither would be the end of the matter. The Church of England must continue to work its way through all aspects of initiation. The re-appraisal of confirmation and the place of the Holy Spirit go hand in hand with a revised baptismal discipline. The fragmentation of the early rite is still a major historical obstacle to be overcome. But if baptismal reform cannot be isolated from its total initiation context, neither must we assume that the complete rite must fall as close to birth as possible. In the New Testament, baptism and the gift of the Spirit came as close to conversion as possible, at whatever age this occurred.

The reform of Anglican infant-baptismal discipline is a task incomplete and long overdue. Granted that major changes take time, the fifty years since Vidler's essay would seem quite long enough to have sorted this one out. Can we hear what the Spirit is saying to our church? I will leave the last word with a baptist, Dr. Beasley-Murray: 'It is possible that this church [the Church of England] will be in the van of baptismal reform within the Church of Christ in Europe, with *unforeseeable consequences for the church in the rest of the world*' (italics mine).[36]

5

A Ghost in the Grove

An exercise in Exorcising
by
Colin Buchanan

Assistant Bishop in the
Diocese of Rochester

A Ghost in the Grove

An exercise in Exorcising

When R. R. Osborn wrote a book called *Forbid Them Not* in 1972, I had already published my own first edition of *Baptismal Discipline*, a very early Grove Booklet, so I was too late to comment in the Grove Booklet on Osborn's book. However, I reached a second edition soon after, and wrote in the introduction that it was astonishing to find a learned parish presbyter in the year of our Lord 1972 still pleading for this policy of administering infant baptism so indiscriminately as to sound more like a writer of 1872.[1] Perhaps I was too easily astonished, for now, at the very point that this present symposium was under discussion, there burst upon us another similar but even more astonishing anachronism, Mark Dalby's *Open Baptism* (1989). King Canute stood against the tide to prove to his flattering courtiers that he could not resist it, but Mark Dalby is obviously determined to turn the tide. So one's astonishment at the untimely character of his cause is matched by the Athanasius-like courage with which he espouses it.

Such a title as *Open Baptism* would attract our attention in any case. So would an argument based (as his is) on the impropriety of getting parents to profess the faith, on the use of godparents as the sole guarantors of the children's upbringing, and on the readiness then to baptise, presumably with no further questions asked, all infants for whom the sacrament is requested. The sense of a ghostly voice from the past, in need of being exorcised, would have been quite strong simply on those grounds. Mark Dalby, however, goes further. He writes as a man who sees himself being more or less steamrollered by modern 'rigorist' approaches. The Lima text is one threat to him (as it certainly should be); 'most modern writers reject even open baptism' (page 5), and that is a further threat. But he does not simply suffer under nameless generalities – he knows who the oppressors are, he names them, and they earn from him a whole chapter of counter-attack and group dismissal. The haunting is specific, targeted, and done with a determination to clear the occupants out of the house. What occupants? Well, there it is in his list of contents: 'Where Grove goes wrong'. Having laid out his position, he is aware (as a ghost from the past must be) that he has laid it out on ground now occupied by others. So he haunts the Grove in the hope of dispossessing the current claimants. And, either for convenience, or through opaqueness of ghostly vision, he lumps Gordon Kuhrt in with 'Grove'. Gordon Kuhrt is, of course, the most respected substantial recent Anglican writer on baptism, in his book, *Believing in Baptism* (Mowbrays, 1987). Well, Gordon, welcome to the Grove – at least if you and I are haunted together, we can share together in exorcising the ghost.

Apart from Gordon Kuhrt's book, the 'Grove' ground is staked out by quotations from various Grove booklets, to which our attention is drawn in Dalby's footnotes on page 95 of *Open Baptism*.[2] It emerges that the ghostly wrath is being poured upon the Grove for the following reasons:

1. '. . . it . . . rejects the concept of the faith of the Church. In other words, Buchanan ignores or rejects the traditional core of the Church of England's apologia which calls so strongly for an open attitude and places such minimal stress on the status of the parents.'[3] We must return below to the issue of parental responsibility.

2. He then deals with the eight lines of biblical argument which make my 'case' for infant baptism[4], and attempts to

show *not* that each of these is a case for baptism within believing households, but that most in principle tend to a more 'open' conclusion than I have drawn from them. This means I must respond, which I have to do by quoting his use of my arguments, and then countering that use with further refutation. So here are the arguments of C.O.B., followed by their changed deployment by Mark Dalby, followed by my refutation of his procedure – it feels like a Reformation disputation:

(i)   I urged that circumcision of a whole nation at birth is not relevant, as Christian faith is not an automatic inheritance. But circumcision in the generations from Abraham to Jacob provides a much better precedent, as in those generations the inheritance was not automatic, but the administering of the rite of circumcision to the children of the believing parents was done to *both* sons in those two generations, without the respective fathers attempting to distinguish the elect from the rejected offspring. Dalby says it is arbitrary to pick those two generations.[5] But although Calvin argued the relevance of the universal circumcision within the land of Judah, he was arguing within a 'Christian' state or commonwealth, which is not our position today. Indeed, Calvin's argument (like most of Dalby's) plays into the hands of the anti-pedobaptist, and, if it apparently confers something as automatic as a dynastic birthright, then it proves too much and sells out to opponents. The argument which relates baptism to circumcision ought to be confined for these purposes to those first two generations (and the New Testament tends to hark back to the first generation of all).

(ii) I argued that, because adults are baptised in the New Testament at the point of professing conversion, and without any apparent probationary period, we have a question as to when children who are going to be brought up as believers within the family of the church should be baptised. My answer was that you cannot treat them properly 'as believers' except by marking and incorporating them at the outset through baptism. Dalby responds that all sorts of infants are going to be brought up as 'Christians' though not very noticeably within the family of the church, and others are going to be brought up in the church through the influence of grandparents and godparents – and that, by parity of argument, these infants should qualify for baptism too. I can only respond: firstly, this particular argument was only raised in relation to believing parents (for that is as far as we can go in confrontation with Baptists, which is part of the context of any argument for infant baptism) – and thus the argument only applies to such parents; secondly, Dalby's definition of unchurched 'Christians' may or may not have some force in our religious mapwork – but by definition it is *not* about that church membership and incorporation which is at the heart of the meaning of baptism; and thirdly, when grandparents and godparents are cited as bringing up children in the church in the faith, then we *have* to have some kind of *post factum* enquiry as to whether godparents and grandparents actually achieve this. Mark Dalby may be ministering in his own parish in some kind of timewarp (perhaps that is exactly what makes him a ghost in the Grove) – but the evidence of four and a half years of ministering confirmation convinces me that his religious parent-substitutes are almost without effect in bringing twelve- and thirteen-year-olds to confirmation.[6]

(iii) I argued that the conversion of 'households' in the New Testament was marked by the baptism of those same households (and indeed that the fullest form of 'missionary baptism' is household baptism). Dalby runs off into an argument that households in the New Testament may include grandchildren, nephews, nieces and young slaves.[7] Thus, by his slippery pattern of argument, because believing heads of households might have qualified more than their own immediate offspring for baptism in the New Testament times, it is 'dangerous' to stake the baptism of infants today upon the faith of parents. But my point is only that the head of an extended household had authority to lead that whole household into baptism (as has been often seen with extended households running as far as whole tribes, in pioneer gospel work in many countries in the centuries since). And my point today would be solely that, as the only 'households' we usually encounter are 'nuclear families', there the head (I do not argue here whether that is one or two parents) has the right and even the duty, when believing and incorporated himself or herself, to take the dependent members of the household into baptism, both at initial conversion, and when further children are born.[8] The argument does not bear upon households where the 'head' does not wish to live life in the family of the church, and, although Dalby says that parents seeking baptism will generally themselves be baptised, it would seem from his instances that he is actually referring to the visibly self-excommunicate.

(iv) On my next two points about the significance (in scripture and in practice) of a 'Christian home', Dalby concedes the argument in principle, and then virtually claims that all homes where at least one parent has been baptised are 'Christian homes', which, he says, 'their subsequent lapsing can never negate'[9]. The situation is self-evidently otherwise.

(v) I then argue that our case for infant baptism would be stronger if we conceded the logic that it should lead into immediate communion – communion to which, obviously, children are brought in tender years by their parents. Dalby, hooked on Prayer Book patterns, does not concede this: 'Church history has put a question-mark against this, and the mark has not yet been removed.'[10] My own discernment would be that the historically conditioned factors which led to the withdrawal of communion from newly baptised infants have been fully exposed *as* historically conditioned and inapplicable today, and that the change in the Church of England's discipline is delayed not through any evenly balanced or unresolved character of the argument but through the sheer inertia in the matter of the House of Bishops.[11]

(vi) I then put in two lightweight arguments, from Acts 2:39 and 1 Corinthians 7:14. Dalby asserts that the Acts passage points in its 'to as many as are far off' to future generations, irrespective almost of faith. I merely affirmed that 'your children' may well have been present, and the adult converts may therefore (especially if proselytes – see Acts 2:11) have followed the logic of their earlier entry into Judaism and, in the light of Peter's words, have then taken their children into Christian baptism with them. 'Those who are far off' has no

obvious reference to children at all. I accept that the 1
Corinthians passage may well not be relevant, for, though its
basis in a 'believing' parent is clear, what is being said about
the consequent 'holiness' of the children is far from clear.

I cannot but be glad that the ghost saw the force of the eight
(cumulative) 'Grove' points, but it will need a much more
persistent haunting than this to prise them loose and detach
them from the Grove. Thus far the force of the haunting has
been derisory.

3. So what of Dalby's own particular points? What will this
    voice from the past have us adopt as sense for the future?

(i)   He is convinced that he is on to something about god-
      parents. He even gives us a tour of scripture to show us
      people undertaking vicarious tasks on behalf of other peo-
      ple. But his main case is in the Prayer Book. There god-
      parents answer 'in the name of this child'; godparents are
      charged (as we have seen) with getting children in due
      course to confirmation; godparents are cited in the catech-
      ism as having so done; and it is what the godparents under-
      took in baptism that the candidates ratify for themselves in
      the confirmation service. I have speculated that, because of
      the medieval run-on of the godparental concept into the
      Reformation, the godparents are actually being addressed
      as *in loco parentis*, and not as persons with substantial duties
      in their own persons, such as to replace the duties of the
      natural parents.[12] But let us take the surface meaning of the
      Prayer Book to be its true meaning as Dalby wants us to. We
      then simply have to ask: is it scriptural? is it credible? is it
      pastoral? is it even possible? The sociological background of
      the 1662 Book was of a rural England where most men and
      women grew up and lived where whey had been born, and
      raised their own families in the same surrounds. Godparents
      might be blood relatives, or might be neighbours – but they
      would in nineteen cases out of twenty be local throughout a
      child's growing years. Let it be that in 1662 a credible
      programme existed of the chosen godparents instructing the
      young children in the faith, taking them to public worship,

urging them into catechism classes, and finally seeing them confirmed. Even if such an idyll can be at least imagined in 1662, it is amazingly unlikely to-day. The nation differs in a dozen definitive respects from Dalby's rural idyll. The basic atmosphere is secular; the average dwelling-place is urban; T.V., the car, divorce, and aircraft have both removed families and godparents from each other, and given them wholly other horizons from those of the past. It is not only absurd to say 'we know these parents may not bring up Willie in the faith, but we are hopeful his godparents will' – but it must surely be transparently absurd to the person himself who says it to himself? There can hardly be evidence that godparents regularly achieve what natural parents fail to. An actual examination of the run-down in confirmation candidates over recent decades must seal the matter. How *can* Dalby believe it himself? He must surely suspect himself of finding a cobbled-up excuse for giving baptism on no conditions whatsoever, and without any regard for plausible boundaries for the church. For, as the ghost waves the Prayer Book at us, we can see 'seventeenth century England' written large across it – and surely he can too?

(ii) The other side of this coin is the conviction that parents should neither undertake anything for the children, nor have to profess anything in their own persons. He makes his case particularly from the seventeenth century, and it is thus compatible with our seventeenth-century Book of Common Prayer. He shows how the Puritans wanted to make a division between believing and unbelieving parents and the bishops would have none of it.[13] But then there was still a background of an ideal of total conformity, a single religion for the whole country, and a unitary church/state kingdom. Infant baptism has a different role in such a case from that which it has to-day, and the seventeenth-century arguments are hardly applicable. The bishops were no doubt also keen at the Savoy Conference to resist every Puritan demand as a matter of principle, and often got themselves on to weak and indefensible ground as a result. But one can well sympathise with their concern about the arbitrariness with which many a Puritan minister would have been separating his parish into sheep and goats by sheer autocratic insight into people's spiritual condition, which might have gone far beyond any-thing that 'rigorists' today would propose. All this detaches the bishops' responses at the Savoy Conference from any relevance to today's conditions. They spoke as men of their times to conditions of their own times.

(iii) This, however, is calculated to touch Dalby on the raw. Because he is a ghost of the seventeenth century, and wants to stick by seventeenth-century principles, he is opposed to the requirement in Series 2 and Series 3 (or A.S.B.) baptis-mal rites that the parents express their own repentance and faith in their own persons. It is a 'great weakness'.[14] And the A.S.B. requirement that parents (and godparents) express their willingness to bring up the child in the faith is worse – 'it appears to make the baptism conditional on the parental response'. And many many twentieth-century pastors would say back 'exactly: that is the biblical basis *and* the rubrical basis of infant baptism in the Church of England today'. We do not necessarily have to investigate too closely how credible the parental profession is (and the degree of investigation will vary from place to place) – but we dare not forego that profession if baptism is to be baptism, and the church of God is to be the church of God. Certainly we cannot follow the beckonings of a ghost and nail our colours to the exact wording and circumstances of 1662, as though we were true contemporaries of his. The ghost inhabited Christendom: we are of missiondom.

So the Grove is unimpressed by the haunting, can learn its seventeenth-century history without feeling forced to live in it, clearly exorcises the ghost, and wants, in the light of scripture, to confront the realities of today.

Epilogue

Quo Vadis, Ecclesia Anglicana?
by
Roger Godin

Management Consultant
Member of the House of Laity

Epilogue

Quo Vadis, Ecclesia Anglicana?

'What evidence I have received suggests that the practical issue now is on what conditions, if any, may Infant Baptism be administered'

Revd. Peter Cornwell
Introducing the debate
on Christian Initiation
19th February 1974

As this book passes to our publishers, we have a sense of muted excitement. Excitement, because as we move into the Decade of Evangelism, those of us who believe that reformation in baptismal policies is a crucial evangelistic issue are encouraged by two developments.

The House of Bishops has commenced a comprehensive study of various issues related to Christian initiation. At the same time as this was announced, it was confirmed that the General Synod Standing Committee had asked for a report to be prepared on the theological, pastoral, evangelistic and ecumenical issues of so-called indiscriminate baptism. Scarcely a week passes without baptismal reform being considered in the secular, let alone religious press. Even the 'Soaps' enter the fray from time to time.

But why is the excitement muted? Because as we will see, the path to baptismal reform is often slower than backwards! Let us follow the process over two decades from the Ely

Report publication in 1971 – the first really exciting document I had seen in General Synod.

This was one of the new breed of Synodical documents that argued first from scripture. With it (at least for the Church of England) came the discovery and recommendation that the Church should make explicit its recognition of baptism as the full and complete rite of Christian initiation. It did not get much applause, actually said little about practical baptismal reform, and to some seemed somewhat confused – even about adult baptism and confirmation.

One of the few tangible things that emerged from the eventual debate in 1974 based also on the supporting paper by Peter Cornwell was this motion . . .

> The General Synod adheres to the view that Infant Baptism should continue to be available to the children of all parents who are **willing and able** to make the requisite promises, [and] asks that the Liturgical Commission should note this expression of view, together with the requirements of Canons B21, B22 and B23, in the framing of any new Baptismal Services.

We will find that the fate of just two words ('and able') exemplify the frustration of the following two decades of debate. Not everyone, even the reformers, thinks these two words, moved by the redoubtable Christopher Wansey, are the panacea of all good things. But whatever their intrinsic merit or otherwise (Colin Buchanan calls them 'perverse' thus underlining our richness of diversity even in the Reform movement!), their history exemplifies the frustrations in the way of reform. Although an appropriate amendment to Canon Law was drawn up that year by Counsel (badly – see later), it 'somehow' remained filed.

There followed a process of consultation in the dioceses not only on the Ely consequentials, but also on the need for new Services of Thanksgiving and/or Blessing of a Child. Nothing much happened synodically until 1976 when as a result of such discussion Synod debated a motion from the

Southwell Diocese which coincidentally happened to house one Colin Buchanan. Whilst 'endorsing the forms of interrogation' in the new services they asked for:

a re-examination of the conditions upon which infants were accepted for baptism.

This gentle request scraped through with a majority of 19 – but what happened as a result? In 1977, a monograph from Canon Knapp-Fisher was issued – but never debated – despite several procedural attempts to resurrect it.

In terms of debate, 1977 *might* have become a watershed for reform. Archdeacon (now Bishop) Peter Dawes had, since 1974, been trying to raise the profile of baptismal services. Frustrated at three previous attempts he at last obtained Synodical approval requiring that baptisms should normally be at a main public service. This was eventually incorporated into Canon B21 –

It is desirable that every minister . . . shall normally administer the sacrament of Holy Baptism on Sundays at public worship when the most number of people come together . . .

Sadly this is ignored by many – even our Royal Family[1] even though the change of wording from 'time-to-time' to 'normally' must make the legal position clear to *any* officiating Minister – be he Curate, Chaplain or Bishop!

But the real opportunities of that year through the introduction of the Series 3 Initiation Services were not taken. Though there was much to welcome, as Mrs. Mayland said in introducing the Liturgical Commission Report,

the Synod has found itself unable to accept the basic tenet of the Ely Report, namely that Baptism is the full and complete rite of Christian Initiation.

So not only the most striking reform of the Ely Report, but also the Southwell Motion remained open issues. Even the 'and able' clause (as yet waiting to find anyone willing and able to project it into Canon Law) had to struggle for survival against a Private Member's motion which appeared in 1980 seeking its removal (only the General Synod could manage a debate seeking removal of something that was not yet there to be removed!), but this motion was heavily defeated.

1981 saw the start of a campaign by Canon Michael Hodge to review the roles of godparents and sponsors in Christian initiation. He was rewarded by yet another monograph, this time by the Bishop of Leicester – but no action. His subsequent attempt in 1985 to ensure the transparently and biblically obvious requirement that even one godparent should be an 'actual communicant member of the Church of England' narrowly failed – some say a victim of the 'tea-room'.

While these internal pressures were achieving little, the Church of England was challenged from outside. Back in 1982 we had been challenged by the Faith and Order Group of the World Council of Churches, in the 'Lima Statement' to respond to this:

> . . . believer baptists and those who practice infant baptism should reconsider certain aspects of their practices. The first may seek to express more visibly the fact that their children are placed under the protection of God's grace. The latter must guard themselves against the practice of apparently indiscriminate baptism and take more seriously the responsibility for the nurture of baptized children to mature commitment to Christ.

There was a careful balance of words used here and in the doctrinal statement preceding. We could perhaps be lulled into apathy by the gentleness of the rebuke. What have we done? There were only ten lines in direct response. Whilst accepting that

> the text is right to warn of the offence which the practice of indiscriminate baptism can cause, where admission to baptism is

granted to those who do not seem to have given any evidence of wanting to be identified with Jesus Christ and his Church –

F.O.A.G. went on only to say that –

> . . . baptismal discipline may be so over-discriminating that those requesting baptism are required to provide unreasonable evidence of the authenticity of their faith. So called 'indiscriminate baptism' reflects a view of the Church as a 'mixed community'; a more rigorous policy emphasises the 'gathered' nature of the Church.

Is it not sad that the 'Concluding Reflections' of our response through F.O.A.G., endorsed by the Synod debate in 1985, made no commitment to undertake pastoral steps to minimise the offence we cause to others? Make no mistake – the word 'apparent' was not there to say *no* offence had been caused!

1985 also saw another attempt for reform pressed by Private Members (it's interesting to reflect on the frequency with which Private Members initiate action – or try to). This was an attempt by Canon Peterken to seek a revival of the ancient concept of the Catechumenate.[2] His motion was only lost because of a perverse wish for a vote by houses, and although achieving a majority overall was lost in the House of Bishops. . . .

A short debate took place in 1986 initiated by Peter Hobson seeking to resuscitate the 1974 '. . . and able' clause again, and it was actually officially admitted that:

> We believed we had taken action synodically against indiscriminate baptism . . . under the impressions that the Canons and A.S.B. rubrics contained the words, relating to godparents . . . 'willing and able' to make the requisite promises . . . The express intention . . . was to rule out indiscriminate baptism . . . Canon B23 was . . . never . . . revised or amended to take account of that Synod resolution . . .

Notice the phrase 'relating to *godparents*'. Even the lawyers got it wrong!

In the meantime I'd got a bit frustrated and, as no one else seemed 'willing', I thought I'd try a Private Member's Motion myself. It was set down in February 1987 when there were not too many others and because it got quite a few signatures, in normal circumstances would have been debated quite quickly. But baptismal reform *is* accident-prone and problems arose – the former Bishop of Bath and Wells had put down his motion requesting Synod to move backwards liturgically (i.e.: 'Let's have a modern English service with old English for the Lord's Prayer'). Then Synod decided that since it was going to move from Church House(!) it MUST say thank you to the owners of the Vitello d'Oro Restaurant when we moved out to Millbank. No one seemed to notice that only the General Synod could praise an Italian Golden Calf!

So at 6.48 p.m. at the fag-end of a heavy day in November 1988, I launched into my opening speech – and the debate was adjourned till February!

On resumption in February 1989 again there was 'trouble at mill'. Suffering yet another adjournment, and after seven amendments of varying degrees of friendliness, a procedural motion to junk the lot, and yet another heavy negative intervention from the Eborian Hobby Horse stables (sadly the jockey departed before several apparently successful unseating attempts), we finally agreed the following:

> This Synod calls attention both to the concern over apparent indiscriminate Baptism, as expressed in the 'Baptism, Eucharist and Ministry' documents, and increasingly shared by many people of differing theological persuasion in the Church of England, and also to the concern felt by others over the theological implications of rigorous Baptism policies, and calls upon the Standing Committee to initiate within the lifetime of this Synod a debate based upon a suitable discussion document concerning current theological, pastoral, evangelistic and ecumenical issues.

Interestingly, the day before the vote came, we were given copies of the Report from the 1988 Lambeth Conference.

This again brought the Church in England the following rebuke:

> We reaffirm the baptism of infants as scriptural deriving in principle from the missionary baptism of households (e.g. Acts 16 15,33), a practice exemplified today in parts of our Communion. The baptism of infants shares as fully in the character of the one baptism as the baptism of adults, but we accept the Lima judgement that indiscriminate infant baptism should not be practised. It obscures the purpose of such baptism, not only from those who request it, but also from those many others who are doubtful about its propriety. Whilst we are aware of the vastly differing contexts in which baptism is sought, we encourage the development of standards and guidelines for the preparation of parents and sponsors, with a view to a common discipline.

So even though one might now have suspected that 'The System' was not really considering baptismal reform urgent and important, it could scarcely ignore the assembled Bishops . . . could it?

I have to say 'accident prone' seems to understate the difficulties in achieving baptismal reform. Suddenly we were informed that there was 'no money' to fund execution of the 1989 'Godin' motion. Subsequently, and only in answer to questions, we were told the cost was £800. (The CBF Chairman was not moved by an offer of private funding, nor others by a less worthy suggestion that the new Secretary General's appointment be delayed to pay for it!) However all was not lost and the Standing Committee, a year after my motion was passed, asked Canon Martin Reardon to Chair a representative 'think tank' and to report back by May 1990. Although the history of monograph responses in this area is not encouraging, I welcome this compromise from the full 'Committee' paper, in view of Martin's wide ecumenical and missionary experience in the Board for Mission and Unity, and because of his commitment to consult widely. In late 1989, after continued pressure, at last the opportunity of amendment through a Miscellaneous Provisions Measure was taken.[3] The first amendment offered had to be amended to make it relate to the proper target – the Parents – and after its modification in Revision Committee (approved *nem con*), it came back to Synod in November 1989 in the following format:

> In Canon B22 (of the baptism of infants) after paragraph 2 there shall be inserted the following paragraph –
> The parents or guardians of an infant to be admitted to Holy Baptism should be willing and able to make such promises as may be required by the form of service to be used for the baptism.

It is interesting to note the words with which the clause was introduced to Synod by the Archdeacon of Oxford in February 1990

> We (in the Revision Committee) were most anxious . . . not to impose conditions that the Church of England has never traditionally imposed, but we accepted that in the England of 1990 it would be normal pastoral responsibility of the minister to see that the parents of the infant concerned were willing and also able in conscience to make any promises that would be required by the form of service to be used.

However once again these innocent little words attracted the BIBB ('Baptism is a British Birthright') brigade. Debate was not possible until July 1990 by which time the Standing Committee had taken two actions to make life more complicated. Firstly to 'be able' to make the affirmations in the ASB service had suddenly become 'Article 7' Business, i.e. it was 'touching doctrinal formulae or the services or ceremonies of the Church of England'. Presumably the existing Canon which must therefore allow people who are 'unable' to make the requisite statements is not a bad thing! Secondly the House of Bishops felt that all discussion should cease until they had completed their own work on all initiation issues including the reading of the Reardon Report.

Why on this matter, does Synod have to wait for the
Bishops (again)? Surely Synod should have what it asked for –
a debate based on the issues in the 1989 Motion covered in the
Reardon Paper (not issued until after the July Synod). That
would then give the Bishops the benefit of the new Synod's
insight first. It sounds so plausible to say 'wait for all the issues
to be covered by the episcopal bench' – what happens often is
that nothing emerges! However the Archbishop of York had
his way in suggesting the Synod adjourn debate. How long
will we wait – another 20 years?

However we are not without some encouragement. A
February 1990 development was the (this time successful)
request in February 1990 from a Private Member's motion
(Peter Hawtin) that the desirability of reviving the
Catechumenate should be considered. On this occasion the
Bishops supported, and at last there is something to encour-
age us – the Bishops do not always say 'No!'.

Since the House of Bishops have themselves announced
that they are committed to a study of all issues related to
initiation, can I offer a few subjects?

(a) A fuller response to BEM;
(b) A pastoral and liturgical response to those who seek some
     liturgical expression of affirmation of baptismal vows taken
     in infancy;
(c) Facing the Ely Report issue of (adult) baptism being the full
     and complete rite of Christian initiation;
(d) Baptismal discipline within the Canon Law;
(e) Communion before Confirmation;
(f) The catechumenate as perhaps a bridge over 'troubled bap-
     tismal waters'.

If the two decades of waiting achieve a rational scripturally
based response to these questions, we will not have decayed
in waiting.

I have learned a lot in these frustrating years.

(a) Such tendentious words as 'rigorist', 'indiscriminate' and 'hosepipe' should now be banned (unless preceded with the apparently disarming 'apparent' adjective); as with other potentially divisive issues, we need to exercise Christian love and acceptance as we seek humbly for truth.

(b) Folk religion still survives – obstinately hindering those who try to lead with their theologically ecumenically sharpened pastoral chins; but its reality needs careful pastoral and episcopal attention.

(c) There even remains a vestige of 'B.C.P. Baptism is British and good' – the B.I.B.B. Brigade referred to earlier. When *will* people at last recognise that this country has moved in the way described in Colin Buchanan's second paragraph?

(d) Theologians can be painful and selective (when did we *ever* get our theology right before taking action: I don't recall that call before A.S.B. was published!).

The sad thing is that when change is properly handled, there is little need for contention.

My wife and I were travelling back from Wales and called in at a few of the small Cotswold churches. We noticed a nicely printed card which said:

'Is Baptism what you want for your child?'

– not very welcoming you might think, but in fact the whole tenor of the card, and I assume the baptismal policy of the Church, was one first of welcome then the offer of Thanksgiving or Baptism. Clearly and unthreateningly, the parents were shown the significance of the alternatives, but left in no doubt at all that first of all, they were welcome.

They were shown the Christian gospel of love and welcome at a time when they are most open to the wonder of a loving Creator God. No question of rejection. As Clifford Owen says, 'Parish Policy' is now the key phrase in understanding baptismal discipline. Increasingly, and I think as never before, the Parishes are beginning to realise the importance to our nation of a coherent policy of baptism.

When this book is published the Reardon Report will be

public – and we must hope and pray that there will be proper debate and informed action. This will require Synodical time and energy. Will the new Synod, in the Decade of Evangelism, at last grasp the opportunity of a responsible review of the Church's initiation rite?

'This is not a pressure group seeking a hearing. It is a spiritual battle whereby the Good News can be shared with those who have never heard the 'Gospel of Christ'.

Notes

1: Foreword

1. The original understanding of this term by those who signed the original MORIB declaration was that norm meant 'the most frequently occurring', and hence the more commonly expected; whilst infant baptism is still the norm in terms of statistics there has been a trend away from this for some time.
2. At the time of going to print Alan has now gone through such a rite and consequently resigned as MORIB's chairman.
3. The phrase 'apparent indiscriminate infant baptism' derives from the *Commentary* (21) in *Baptism, Eucharist and Ministry* (W.C.C. Geneva 1982) in which reference is made to the way in which infant baptism tends to be administered in the majority of European and North American churches.

2: A Parish Priest Looks at Baptism

1. Flemington, Beasley-Murray et alia.
2. Beasley-Murray, *Baptism in the New Testament*, p. 14.
3. A Christian is a disciple of Jesus – see Acts 11:26b.
4. ASB p.245.
5. Jeremias, *Infant Baptism in the First Four Centuries*.
6. ASB p.213.
7. Jeremias, *Infant Baptism*.

3: Infant Baptism – the Atomised Sacrament

1. Water baptism is not recorded in every case of conversion in the Acts of the Apostles, but it was clearly part of the *kerygma*, and was given at the point of conversion (cf. Acts 2, Acts 10, Acts

16, etc.); similarly in Paul's letters to the young churches, it is taken for granted that all to whom the letters are addressed had received it (cf. Rom. 6:3–6; 1 Cor. 10:1, 12:13; Gal. 3:27 etc.). Thus we conclude that it was always given at conversion – and sooner rather than later (cf. Acts 8:36–39, Acts 10:47,48 etc.).

2. The present tendency is to think converts need breaking into active ministry slowly – in the New Testament they were expected to testify on the spot!

3. 'Bring them up in the nurture and admonition of the Lord' (Eph. 6:4) is very much part of the argument for infant baptism – children are to grow up 'in' it, not 'unto' it. For a fullish biblical case see my *A Case for Infant Baptism* (Grove Books, Bramcote, 1973, 4/1990).

4. Hippolytus, *Apostolic Tradition*, chapter 21, in G. J. Cuming (ed.) *Hippolytus: A Text for Students* (Grove Books, Bramcote, 1976, 4/1987) pp.18–21.

5. Tertullian, *De Baptismo*, chapter 18, in E. Evans (ed.) *Tertullian's Homily on Baptism* (SPCK, London, 1964 pp.36–41.

6. The alternative explanation is that infant baptism itself was an innovation in Tertullian's time. This view can *just* be propounded, through the paucity of other earlier specific evidence. But, in days when innovation was self-condemned, and tradition had to be sustained and maintained, it is almost unthinkable that, if infant baptism had started during Tertullian's own lifetime, he would not have denounced it simply on that basis. A slowly shifting rationale for an apostolic rite is a hundred times easier to believe than a latterday invention of infant baptism itself.

7. I confess I have never checked this, but rely upon the *obiter dicta* of George Every when he was teaching at Kelham – 'In the Middle Ages, the majority of baptisms in England were done by midwives.'

8. Baptising all children was part of the *cuius regio, eius religio* doctrine which in England found its expression in the nationalisation or 'establishing' of the Church of England. Because they still had no 'missionary' church – and because they were rediscovering 'justification through faith' – individual benefits were as far as they could usually get. (But note the opening of Article xxiv of the Forty-Two Articles of 1553: 'Our Lord Jesus Christ hath knit together a company of new people with sacra-

ments, most few in number, most easy to be kept, most excellent in signification, as is Baptism, and the Lord's Supper'). And although the Hussites had been keen to restore child communion (cf. David Holeton, *Infant Communion Then and Now* (Grove Books, Bramcote, 1980), the more general reformation view was that the ability to answer catechetical questions correctly was crucial for admission to communion (cf. my *Anglican Confirmation* (Grove Books, Bramcote, 1986) pp.19–22).

9. 1549, 1552, and 1559 permitted lay persons to give baptism when there was '*great need*'. The Puritans objected at the Hampton Court Conference ('baptism not to be ministered by women'), and the titles of the rite and the rubric were altered. Now '*the minister of the parish*' or '*any other lawful minister that can be procured*' is to officiate (all italics my emphasis).

10. To put it at its most paradoxical – an unbeliever would do as a witness, and an excommunicate would benefit by being put in remembrance of his own baptism. Indeed, we might add, even a believer in good standing needs to be put in remembrance of his or her own baptism on a regular basis, and not simply in accord with the unpredictable fertility rate of the parish . . .

11. 'Baptist' is a tricky word, but I use it not to mean members of a particular denomination, but to cover all those opposed to infant baptism. It will be clear upon reflection that a highly 'voluntarist' doctrine of the church marches alongside their position on baptism, and the two reinforce each other.

12. Some of the tension of trying to make the church credible *as* the church without giving it credible baptismal boundaries can be found in the Swanwick Conference papers, Basil Moss (ed.) *Crisis for Baptism* (S.C.M., 1965). There were, of course some who resolved the tension – compare the over-reaction of Christopher Wansey (who gave up all baptising of infants, and invented – for Anglicans – the post-natal dry run).

13. See P. A. Crowe (ed.), *Keele '67* (Falcon, 1967) *passim*.

14. Part of my own experience of this was in writing *Baptismal Discipline* (Grove Booklet on Ministry and Worship no. 3 – published in March 1972 originally, and now succeeded by no. 98, *Policies for Infant Baptism*, of January 1987). Then came the diocesan debates responding to the Ely Report in the years 1974–76, at the end of which I successfully moved in General

Synod the Southwell diocesan motion, affirming the form of vows in Series 2 infant baptism and (draft) Series 3 infant baptism rites, and asking for a re-consideration of the terms on which infants were accepted for baptism. This was followed by almost total inaction – see Roger Godin's chapter for an account of it. The form of the baptismal vows I discuss in my own chapter on Mark Dalby's book.

15. Even as I write this, Michael Saward has published figures showing that in London dioceses now, only 11% of children born live receive infant baptism from the Church of England. Whilst some of the decline is no doubt due to parish policies (he shows a widespread desire among the clergy for a tightening of policies), the larger part is almost certainly due to the multi-religious and wholly irreligious character of so many London-ers, and the 'folklore' instinct towards baptism is fading from the urban scene. (At that, if even 11% of live births represented active future church membership, well, the kingdom would be showing signs of coming in London . . .)

16. There are of course other demanding reasons why the establish-ment should be ended – not least in relation to the political factors involved in the choosing of our chief pastors.

4: Grasping the Nettle

1. Philip Crowe, *Christian Baptism* (Mowbrays 1980).
2. Bridge and Phypers (Inter-Varsity Press, Leicester 1977).
3. See also Hugh N. Carson, *Farewell to Anglicanism* (Henry E. Walter 1969). Carson resigned as Vicar of St Paul's, Cambridge and from the Anglican ministry on a number of related issues of which baptismal practice was the chief.
4. Alec Vidler, 'Baptismal Disgrace', *Theology*, vol. xli (1940), p.8.
5. J. R. H. Moorman, Rector of Fallowfield, Manchester and later Bishop of Ripon; author of works on St Francis of Assisi.
6. Cyril E. Pocknee (Mowbrays 1962).
7. Christopher Wansey has gone into much more detail in *The Clockwork Church* (see note 24).
8. Paul Welsby, *History of the Church of England, 1945–80* (O.U.P. 1984), p.62.

9. S.P.C.K. 1955.
10. The view expressed by Dr. Mason and Dom. Gregory Dix that the Holy Spirit is basically given in confirmation.
11. Macmillan 1966.
12. The full report of the conference is published in *Crisis for baptism*, Ed. Basil J. Moss (S.C.M. 1965).
13. The Church of England Liturgical Commission had apparently suggested this in its 1958 report.
14. This fourth motion is substantially the position of MORIB (Movement for the Reform of Infant Baptism) founded in 1986.
15. *Christian Initiation:* Birth and Growth in Christian Society, *The Ely Report* (G.S.30 1971).
16. G.S. 184, January (1974).
17. Peter Jagger, *Christian Initiation in the Church of England. Some radical recommendations*, Church Union Pamphlet (1975).
18. See Sykes and Booty, *The Study of Anglicanism*, chapter 4 on Initiation, by David Holeton, p.268.
19. G.S. 184, p.9 para.18.
20. Colin Buchanan, *Baptismal Discipline*, Grove Booklet 3 (1974).
21. ibid, p.6.
22. Ely Report p.35.
23. In Guildford Diocese, at a rural deans' meeting 1984.
24. See Christopher Wansey's *The Clockwork Church* (Becket Publications, 1978).
25. M. Botting, *Teaching the Families* (C.P.A.S. 1969) p.81.
26. *Baptismal Discipline*, p.21.
27. See 'Do you do christenings?' by Mark Silversides in *A Workbook on Popular Religion* Ed. E. Bailey (Partners Publication 1986).
28. Wesley Carr, *Brief Encounters, Pastoral Ministry through the occasional offices* (SPCK 1985).
29. ibid, p.87.
30. It can hardly be this as all baptismal rites make it clear that the sacrament is administered in the context of a profession of repentance and faith.
31. I am not attempting in this essay to do more than hint at the wider discussion of the relation of baptism to confirmation and first communion.

32. Categories 4 and above on my schematic diagram.
33. Gordon Kurht, *Believing in Baptism* (Mowbrays 1987) devotes a chapter 9 to the case for discrimination in baptism.
34. Colin Buchanan, *Baptismal Discipline*, p.17 last para.
35. Peter Jagger, *The future of Christian initiation in the Church of England – Catholic or Compromise* (Church Union 1975) p.11.
36. C. Beasley-Murray, *Baptism today and tomorrow* (Macmillan, London 1966).

5: A Ghost in the Grove

1. R. R. Osborn, *Forbid Them Not* (SPCK, London, 1972).
2. The booklets cited are as follows: *Baptismal Discipline* (Ministry and Worship no. 3, 1972, and 1974); *A Case for Infant Baptism* (Ministry and Worship no. 20, 1973, 1978, 1983, and 1990); *The Liturgy for Infant Baptism (Series 3)* (Ministry and Worship no. 37, 1975 – this was a commentary on a draft text which never proceeded further, and the booklet is long out of print); *Policies for Infant Baptism* (Worship Series no. 98, 1987 – the booklet which replaces *Baptismal Discipline*). In addition to these the following also bear on baptismal issues, but are not cited: (Jointly with David Pawson) *Infant Baptism under Cross-examination* (Ministry and Worship no. 24, 1974, 1978, and 1983); *One Baptism Once* (Ministry and Worship no. 61, 1978, 1983, and 1989); *Liturgy for Initiation: The Series 3 Services* (Ministry and Worship no. 65, 1979); *ARCIC and Lima on Baptism and Eucharist* (Grove Worship Series no. 86, 1983); *Adult Baptism* (Worship Series no. 91, 1985); *Anglican Confirmations* (Grove Liturgical Study no. 48, 1986).
3. Mark Dalby, *Open Baptism* (SPCK, 1989) p.82.
4. *Policies for Infant Baptism*, p.3.
5. Dalby, *op. cit.* p.83.
6. The Prayer Book rite for Public Baptism of Infants charges godparents to see that the child is duly catechised and presented to the bishop for confirmation, and Dalby lays great weight on this (whereas I would want to investigate both the meaning and the relevance of such a charge to godparents today). Thus, for the purposes of his argument, the situation cries out for actual

scrutiny of the success rate – which is what I think he would condemn as 'sociological' (p.84)!

7. Dalby, *op. cit.* p.85.
8. I should add that there *are* other 'households' today quite apart from 'nuclear families', of which a Christian orphanage would be a most obvious example.
9. Dalby *op. cit.* p.85.
10. *idem*.
11. I was a member of the 'Knaresborough' working party which reported in 1985 in the substantial (and unanimous) document *Communion before Confirmation?* (Church Information Office, 1985). This had one General Synod debate on the motion to 'take note' of it in November 1985, and has since lain untouched on the shelves of the House of Bishops, who now at last have (in January 1990) indicated their hope of bringing the issue forward to the General Synod in 1991. Generations of children put out their hands hopefully, but then through sheer tarrying reach confirmation age whilst the House of Bishops does precisely nothing. See my *Children in Communion* (Grove Books, Bramcote, 1990), pp.20–22.
12. See my *Liturgy for Initiation*, p.25.
13. Dalby *op. cit.* pp.48–51.
14. Dalby *op. cit.* p.98 and elsewhere.

Epilogue: Quo Vadis, Ecclesia Anglicana?

1. The Royal Family are of course a fine example of regular churchgoing, but it would be nice if the next family Christenings were to take place in the main public worship services at Sandringham or Windsor. – Ed.
2. To define this somewhat shadowy concept as between reception into the fellowship support ('the Church embraces') and membership by baptism is perhaps a little inadequate, but gives hope for common ground in future baptismal policies.
3. It is important to note, as stated by Oswald Clarke in introducing the Measure, that 'It is . . . of the essence of Miscellaneous Provisions Measures that the proposals with which it deals are uncontroversial or at least are thought to be substantially uncontroversial'.

Select Bibliography

Aland, K. *Did the Early Church Baptise Infants?* S.C.M., London, 1963

Baillie, J. *Baptism and Conversion*, O.U.P., London, 1964

Barth, K. *The Teaching of the Church regarding Baptism* (translated E. A. Payne), S.C.M., London, 1948

Beasley-Murray, G. R. *Baptism in the New Testament*, Eerdmans, Grand Rapids, Michigan, 1962/1984
Baptism Today and Tomorrow, Macmillan, London, 1966

Beckwith, R. T. 'Infant Baptism', in C. Brown (ed.), *New International Dictionary of New Testament Theology*, Paternoster, Exeter, 1975

Beckwith, R. T., Buchanan, C. O., Prior, K. (eds.) *Services of Baptism and Confirmation*, Marcham, Abingdon, 1967

Bridge, D. and Phypers, D. *The Water that Divides*, IVP, Leicester, 1977

British Council of Churches, *Report of the Inter-church Enquiry into Baptismal Practice*, BCC, London, n.d.
One Lord, one Faith, one Baptism: Guidelines and Materials for Inter-church Worship, BCC, London, n.d.

Bromiley, G. *Children of Promise*, Eerdmans, Grand Rapids, 1979

Buchanan, C. O. *Baptismal Discipline*, Grove, Nottingham, 1972/4
A Case for Infant Baptism, Grove, Nottingham, 1973, 1990
Adult Baptisms, Grove, Nottingham, 1985
(ed.), *Evangelical Essays on Church and Sacraments*, SPCK, London, 1972
Policies for Infant Baptism, Grove, Nottingham, 1987
One Baptism Once, Grove, Nottingham, 1978, 1989
Liturgy for Initiation, Grove, Nottingham, 1979
Anglican Confirmation, Grove, Nottingham, 1986

ARCIC and LIMA on Baptism and Eucharist, Grove, Nottingham, 1983

Carey, G. 'Christian beginning', ch. 5 of J. R. W. Stott (ed.), *Obeying Christ in a Changing World*, Vol. 1, *The Lord Christ*, Collins, Glasgow, 1977

Carr, W. *Brief Encounters*, SPCK, London, 1985

Craston, R. C. *Baptism*, BCMS, London, n.d.

Crowe, P. *Christian Baptism*, Mowbray, Oxford, 1980

Cullmann, O. *Baptism in the New Testament* (translated by J. K. S. Reid), S.C.M. London, 1950

Dalby, M. *Open Baptism*, SPCK, 1989

Davies, J. K. *Babies, Believers and Baptism*, Grace, London, 1983

Dunn, J. D. G. *Baptism in the Holy Spirit*, S.C.M., London, 1970
'Baptism' in *The illustrated Bible Dictionary*, IVP, Leicester, 1980

Eastman, A. T. *The Baptizing Community*, Seabury, Minnesota, 1982

Ely Report *Christian Initiation: Birth and Growth in the Christian Society*, CIO, London, 1971

Faith and Order Advisory Group (Board for Mission and Unity), *Toward a Church of England Response to BEM and ARCIC*, CIO, London, 1985

Flemington, W. F. *The New Testament Doctrine of Baptism*, SPCK, London, 1948/1957

Forsyth, P. T. *The Church and the Sacraments*, Independent, London, 1917/1947

Gilmore, A. (ed.) *Christian Baptism*, Lutterworth, London, 1959
Baptism and Christian Unity, Lutterworth, London, 1966

Green, E. M. B. *I believe in the Holy Spirit*, Hodder, London, 1975
Baptism, Hodder, London, 1987

Hart, G. *Right to Baptize*, Hodder, London, 1966

Holeton, D. 'The Study of Anglicanism' in Sykes and Booty (eds.), *The Study of Anglicanism*, SPCK, 1988

Jagger, P. J. *Clouded Witness, Initiation in the Church of England 1850/1875*, Pickwick, 1982

Jeremias, J. *Infant Baptism in the First Four Centuries*, S.C.M., London, 1960
The Origins of Infant Baptism, S.C.M., London, 1963

Jewett, P. K. Infant Baptism and the Covenant of Grace, Eerdmans, Grand Rapids, 1978

Knaresborough Report, *Communion before Confirmation?* CIO, London, 1985

Kuhrt, G. *Believing in Baptism*, Mowbray, 1987

Lampe, G. W. H. *The Seal of the Spirit*, SPCK, London, 1951/67

Lane, E. *I Want to be Baptised*, Grace, London, 1986

Marcel P. *The Biblical Doctrine of Infant Baptism* (translated by P. E. Hughes), 1951/1953

Moody, D. *Baptism: Foundation for Christian Unity*, Westminster Press, Philadelphia, 1967

Moore, G. and Briden T. *Moore's Introduction to England Canon Law*, Mowbray, Oxford, 1985

Moss, B. S. (ed.) *Crisis for Baptism*, S.C.M., London, 1965

Murray, J. *Christian Baptism*, Philadelphia, 1952

Ogilvie, G. *Preaching at Baptisms*, Grove, Nottingham, 1979

Osborn, R. R. *Forbid them not*, SPCK, London, 1972

Packer, J. I. *I want to be a Christian*, Kingsway, Eastbourne, 1977

Pawson, D. and Buchanan, C. O. *Infant Baptism under Cross-examination*, Grove, Nottingham, 1974

Pawson, J. D. *The Normal Christian Birth*, Hodder, 1989

Quick, O. C. *The Christian Sacraments*, Nisbet, London, 1927/1932

Richardson, A. 'Initiation, Christian' in A. Richardson (ed.), *A Dictionary of Christian Theology*, S.C.M., London, 1969

Robinson, D.W.B. *The Meaning of Baptism*, Falcon, London, 1956

Scotland, Church of, *The Biblical Doctrine of Baptism*, St Andrew, Edinburgh, 1958

Silversides, M. *Folk Religion: Friend or Foe?* Grove, Nottingham, 1986

Southwell Diocesan Working Party, *Report on policies concerning Infant Baptism*, Grove, Nottingham, 1977

Stott, J. R. W. 'The Evangelical Doctrine of Baptism', Ch. 6 of W. R. F. Browning (ed.), *The Anglican Synthesis*, Peter Smith, Derby, 1964

Sykes and Booty (eds.), *The Study of Anglicanism* (art. by David Holeton) – SPCK, 1988

Thurian, M. *Ecumenical Perspectives on Baptism, Eucharist and Ministry*, WCC, Geneva, 1983

Wainwright, G. *Christian Initiation*, Lutterworth, London, 1969

Wansey, C. *The Clockwork Church*, Becket, 1978

Watson, T. E. *Baptism not for Infants*, 1962

Whitaker, E. C. *Sacramental Initiation complete in Baptism*, Grove, Nottingham, 1975

White, R. E. O. *The Biblical Doctrine of Initiation*, Hodder, London, 1960

Williams, R. R. 'Baptism' in A. Richardson (Ed.), *A Theological Wordbook of the Bible*, S.C.M., London, 1960

World Council of Churches Commission on Faith and Order, *One Lord, one Baptism*, S.C.M., London, 1960

World Council of Churches, Faith and Order Paper: 111, *Baptism, Eucharist and Ministry (The Lima text)*, WCC, Geneva, 1982

Wright, D. F. *Baptism, Eucharist and Ministry: an evangelical assessment*, Rutherford Forum Paper, Edinburgh, 1984

Acknowledgement:

I am grateful to Mrs. Anne Gaydon of Clifton-on-Teme for sorting and typing this bibliography.

BAPTISM

Michael Green

"Therefore go and make disciples of all nations, baptising them in the name of the Father and of the Son and of the Holy Spirit."

Baptism: as an infant, as a believer, and by the Holy Spirit. Michael Green provides a bold, clear explanation of the different approaches, examining the biblical evidence and teaching. Common ground between the churches is emphasised, along with the insistence that baptism is no substitute for saving faith in believers. Even so, the author's conviction of the validity and benefits of infant baptism, in appropriate circumstances, is presented with energy and thoroughness.

This popular account will help many to a deeper understanding of the real significance of baptism.

INNER CITY GOD

Geoffrey Ahern & Grace Davie

Opinion polls suggest that over seventy per cent of people in Britain actually believe in God, yet barely ten per cent attend church with any regularity. INNER CITY GOD throws light on this apparent discrepancy through its sociological study into the extent and nature of belief in the inner city.

Geoffrey Ahern, from the Alister Hardy Research Centre in Oxford, allows us to savour the experiences and attitudes of 'us' and 'them' as he summarises his research into the beliefs of white, working-class, non-church-going inhabitants of Tower Hamlets in East London, and 'them': twelve Anglican clergymen. Grace Davie, who has lived in Liverpool for sixteen years, develops her work for the Archbishop's Commission on Urban Priority, as she examines the different strands of 'common' or 'natural' religion, and considers whether the variety of beliefs, superstitions and misapprehensions makes the churches' task more difficult. Andrew Walker introduces the 'problem' of the inner city, and draws out the key issues which arise from these studies. Research for INNER CITY GOD was co-ordinated by the C. S. Lewis Centre.

'I was brought up with a jolt . . . An honest attempt to examine religious attitudes in urban areas . . . We ignore natural religion at our peril. A particular dread of mine is that those who feel themselves excluded from successful, organised life come to see the church as yet one more authority.'
Bishop David Sheppard in his foreword.

GOD OF OUR FATHERS

Frank Colquhoun

GOD OF OUR FATHERS reveals the breadth of our island spirituality, and is invaluable as a devotional and bedside book, a help to the study of the development of prayers, and a wide-ranging reference source.

Frank Colquhoun has assembled a well researched and inspired collection of prayers which clearly reveal the concerns, attitudes and underlying faith of the Church in Britain and Ireland, both past and present.

The prayers have been grouped in sections covering the earlier centuries (up to the 15th century), the Reformation and Elizabethan periods, the 17th and 18th centuries, and the present century.

Canon Frank Colquhoun is an acknowledged authority on liturgical prayers and hymns. Now retired, he lives with his wife in Bexhill-on-Sea. He has compiled the highly successful series PARISH PRAYERS, NEW PARISH PRAYERS and CONTEMPORARY PARISH PRAYERS, as well as many other books.

EVANGELISM THROUGH THE LOCAL CHURCH

Michael Green

As we enter the Decade of Evangelism, Michael Green contends that to be successful evangelism must be rooted in the total involvement of the local church and in terms that are meaningful in today's largely secular society.

EVANGELISM THROUGH THE LOCAL CHURCH tackles the current challenge presented by the secular world. The biblical mandate for evangelism is defined, and church-based evangelism is detailed – in all its diversity. EVANGEL-ISM THROUGH THE LOCAL CHURCH is the fruit of a lifetime's work as an evangelist, pastor and teacher.

'Michael Green has put his finger on the vital link for restoring Christian witness in this secular age.'

Charles Colson

'For sustained reflection on this urgent topic, and for massive practical experience, few could rival Michael Green.'

Robert Runcie, Archbishop of Canterbury

Michael Green, for many years rector of St Aldate's, Oxford, is currently Professor of Evangelism at Regent College, Vancouver. He is the editor of the Jesus Library and I Believe series, and the author of BAPTISM, and MATTHEW FOR TODAY.